NATIONAL BESTSELLER

foreword by **Greg S Reid**

treasure map
to

ONE WOMAN'S JOURNEY
FROM DISRUPTION TO JOY

Stacie Shifflett

Treasure Map to Joy™
One Woman's Journey from Disruption to Joy
Stacie Shifflett

Copyright © 2025
Stacie Shifflett

ISBN: 979-8-9927569-4-4

Joint Venture Publishing

The Millionaire Mentor, Inc.

dedication

For my younger self—
the one who was still searching,
still proving,
still trying to remember what she already knew.
I didn't have a map.
But I forged a path ahead anyway.

Sometimes I fumbled.
Sometimes I triumphed.
Sometimes I got lost.
And sometimes I dug deeply
into the well of my soul to change course.

Life was full of surprises.
Some welcome. Some not.

Yet here I stand.
Molding my hard-won wisdom
into something shareable—
something useful—
so that another woman might light her own path
with a little more grace,
and a lot more clarity.

table of contents

foreword

Throughout the centuries, people have dreamed of finding hidden treasures, ornate chests filled with precious metals, rare gems, ancient coins, and historic artifacts. But the dream rarely becomes a reality because few have ever held a map that will lead them to such a monumental discovery.

In this book, however, you hold a map to an even bigger treasure — the joy that is uniquely yours. And it is not just for a select few — joy is attainable for everyone. It doesn't have to be earned and requires no digging, drilling, or metal detectors. The only tool needed is awareness of what brings you joy and the willingness to intentionally pursue it.

What brings you joy? Is it good health and wellness? Maybe your joy is in accomplishing major goals or milestones, like earning a master's degree, landing a dream job, or climbing Mt. Kilimanjaro. Perhaps your greatest joy is in finally running a marathon or walking into the sunset with the love of your life. Whether your joy is derived from your career, your relationships, or your surroundings, it is unique to you, and, therefore, you are the only one who holds the key to unlock it.

It is said that you cannot hit a target that you cannot see, and that is true in your quest for joy. In this book, Stacie Shifflett reveals how you can identify the pivotal areas that are missing in your life, so you can take steps that will lead you directly to them. As a coach, she has guided clients toward a life they once only dreamed about—a life filled with passion, purpose, and joy.

From the first time we met, I have been impressed by Stacie's mind. She is passionate, creative, and never lacking for new ways to make a positive difference in the lives of others through her company and philosophy, Modern Consciousness®. A multi-faceted entrepreneur, her program, Elevate Your Life®, is a guide through the art of transformation that leads people to the life they truly love.

Treasure Map to Joy™ takes you along for that journey. You'll meet Maureen, a woman who is facing multiple life challenges, and Leina, her coach, who guides her on the journey of a lifetime. As the pages turn, Maureen follows a path of self-discovery and transformation that paves the way to fulfillment and happiness.

Joy is, indeed, the ultimate treasure in life, and everyone can claim it. Let this book lead the way and embark on your journey today … your treasure awaits.

Greg S. Reid
Bestselling Author and
Founder of Secret Knock

introduction

If someone handed you a map to life's greatest treasure, would you set sail on a voyage to discover the secrets within?

I'm not talking about searching for ancient artifacts, gold, or diamonds. The treasure I'm referring to is far more valuable — and far more elusive. It's the kind no one else can claim because it's uniquely yours: your own Treasure Map to Joy™.

If you had such a map, would you follow it? Would you venture into the unknown to discover the fulfillment that waits at the other end of that journey?

Throughout my life, I've seen my path as a kind of adventure — one filled with twists, turns, and new beginnings. I've reinvented myself many times across different careers and industries, including hospitality, technology, and construction. I even owned a llama farm! Reinvention came easily to me; it was simply part of who I was. But not every change in life is one we choose.

When my infant son died, the grief was unbearable. Yet the foundation of my life — my marriage, my home, my work — remained intact, and it was that stability that carried me through the pain.

Years later, though, my divorce shattered that structure completely. It wasn't just the loss of a marriage; it was the unraveling of everything familiar. That's when I found myself questioning not only what I wanted, but who I truly was.

That moment became the turning point — the real beginning of my personal growth journey. It's what ultimately led me to the deeper work of rediscovering joy and creating what would become *Modern Consciousness*® and *Treasure Map to Joy*™.

So, let me ask you: What treasure are you seeking?

Do you believe it exists?

And if so, how far are you willing to go to find it?

Over the years, I've come to believe that peace of mind is our greatest personal asset — the real treasure at the heart of a fulfilling life. When we have peace of mind, joy naturally rises to meet it. But peace doesn't appear by chance; it's cultivated through awareness, understanding, knowledge, and what is so often the missing piece — *right action*.

That's the work of this book.

In these pages, you'll witness what becomes possible when someone dares to look within, trusts her own compass, and takes action. Her journey reveals that transformation isn't about perfection — it's about perspective, courage, and choice.

Because ultimately, the miracle you've been waiting for… is you.

So, as we embark on this journey together, ask yourself not only what treasures you seek, but how ready you are to chart the course to reach them.

Let's set sail. Your adventure begins now.

1

There was a quiet nervousness when Maureen arrived at her office on Monday morning.

"Hey, Maureen, check your email," her coworker, Lynda, whispered in her ear as she passed by.

Those weren't the only hushed conversations Maureen noticed as she went to the kitchenette to fill her coffee cup while her computer was booting up.

"Good morning," she smiled when she entered.

"We'll see about that," Gavin sarcastically replied.

Curious, she returned to her desk and logged into her email account. It wasn't difficult to find what the buzz was about as the subject line was in all caps: MANDATORY MEETING.

She opened the email from the Vice President of Human Resources, notifying them that everyone was required to attend a meeting about possible restructuring of the company on Friday morning at 9:00 a.m. sharp. It didn't surprise Maureen at all. In fact, she'd been expecting it. Everyone knew that the company's stock had taken a hit with the downturn of the economy. It made sense to Maureen that changes would have to be made, but she believed the company was stable enough it could weather the storm. Understandably, restructuring made sense, even if it was a temporary move. So, while some of her coworkers felt a measure of anxiety, she wasn't too worried. Like her mother had always said, "This, too, shall pass."

That was a phrase Maureen had reminded herself of more times than she wished in the past few years. At 52 years old, she thought her life would have been more stable than ever, and it should have been. She and her husband had become empty nesters after spending 22 years raising their daughter and son—a time when many couples look forward to the opportunity to rediscover themselves and devote the time to each other that had taken a backseat to raising kids. To Maureen's surprise, though, her husband became isolated and disinterested, preferring to spend his free time at the golf course. When they were home together and she attempted to talk about their future, his responses were noncommittal, even aloof.

One day, she'd finally had enough and came right out and asked him what was wrong.

"The kids are gone, and we can finally do everything we've talked about for years. But it doesn't seem like you even want to talk about it anymore. It feels like you don't even want to talk at all. What's up, David?"

He didn't even skip a beat before flatly replying, "I want out."

"What do you mean?" she asked.

"I'm not happy. I want a divorce," he announced.

Blindsided, she tried to reason with him.

"We just have to adjust to life without the kids. Maybe it's a mid-life crisis. That's normal. We can get through this—we've gotten through worse. Let's go to counseling and work through this together. I'll learn how to golf…"

He interrupted before she could finish.

"I'm sorry, Maureen. It's over."

And with that, he checked out. After a few days of uncomfortable silence, she came home from work one day to find his bags were packed.

"This is all I need for now," he said before walking away as if she was a stranger, not his wife of 27 years and the mother of his children.

For the first time, Maureen found herself alone. The hardest part was living in a house full of memories. Every room reminded her of a period in their busy lives—the pitter patter of their babies' feet as they learned to walk, the corner by the fireplace where they put the Christmas tree and took a family photo every year, the front porch where she'd envisioned they'd sit and relax in their golden years…

When the For Sale sign went up in the front yard, she reminded herself that it was just a house, no longer a home. Knowing there would be no more memories made there, she spent long evenings and weekends alone going through their belongings, separating what was his and what was hers, the past from the future.

Maureen moved into the first townhouse her realtor showed her. It wasn't anything special, but then again, she didn't need much. She had no wish list—quartz or granite countertops didn't matter. It was just another house, but it was a far cry from a home.

Work became her therapy, and she threw herself into it, accepting extra projects and working into the evenings. Her dedication was noticed, and she accepted a promotion to the position of senior data analyst. In a different time, she would have celebrated the recognition and accomplishment, but there wasn't anyone to celebrate with, although her children did send her flowers with a card that simply said, "Congratulations, Mom!"

Since then, her ex-husband had married his 36-year-old girlfriend, while Maureen chose to be married to her job. That was why she wasn't too stressed about the meeting — whatever happened, she could adapt. With 13 years at the company, she'd climbed the ladder and had the seniority to guarantee job security in the event there would be layoffs. She'd continue to give the company everything she had until they were firmly on their feet once again.

***

The entire department had assembled on Friday morning, and the room fell silent when the president of the company and the director of human resources walked to the front of the room. Suddenly, Maureen could feel a shift in the atmosphere — a formal seriousness that she hadn't seen before. No time was wasted before she learned why.

"At 3:00 yesterday afternoon, our company was purchased by Roberts Enterprises. We have been instructed to cease operations and clear the premises by the end of the working day. Shannon from HR is here to provide each of you with information about insurance and other benefits. There are boxes in the breakroom you can use for your personal belongings," the president said. "After you clean out your desks, you are free to leave. Good luck."

For the second time in the last three years, Maureen was blindsided. She felt like someone had knocked the wind out of her. Numb, she followed her coworkers into the breakroom and retrieved a box. Some were visibly upset, and she noticed a few tears. A few were angry that the company would treat them with such disregard … "After all I've done for them!" Maureen, on the other hand, didn't say a word. She still couldn't believe this was happening.

Sighing, she sat the box on her desk and placed her coffee cup into it. Then she went through every drawer in her desk, but to her surprise, there wasn't anything in or on her desk that belonged to her — no family pictures, no inspirational posters, no memories of her years at the company she could take with her. Then she spotted a leather-bound planner that her daughter had given her for Christmas the year before. Picking it up, she flipped through the pages, only to find that it was empty.

As she pulled into her driveway, she picked up the box, containing only an empty coffee cup and an empty planner, and it wasn't lost on her that she was taking them into a house that was just as empty.

She'd always envisioned that her last day at the company would be the day she retired. It would be a day of joy and new beginnings.

Ironically, there was less joy in her life than there were items in the box. And the blank planner told her that tomorrow would be no different.

2

Time was the one thing Maureen had plenty of, and she found the days to be long. She contemplated taking a trip to visit her children, but when she brought it up, they both said it wasn't a good time. Sophie, her daughter, had agreed to be her best friend's maid of honor, and they were in the midst of wedding planning. And her son, Jake, informed her that he was planning a ski trip with his buddies.

"But we'll get together soon, Mom. I promise," he assured her.

It occurred to her that it might be a good time to take a cruise. After all, she'd never taken one before. It was another one of those things that would happen one day, one among many of the plans and dreams that were wiped out when her husband left.

Then, reality set in, and Maureen reminded herself that she didn't have a job. With no income coming in, she needed to stretch her bank account as far as possible. It wouldn't be responsible for her to take a cruise right now, and if Maureen had been anything in the past, it was responsible.

So, she fell into a daily routine of searching job openings and sending resumes, followed by a daily walk before going back home to make a quick dinner for one. After cleaning up her dishes, the TV or a book kept her company until it was time to go to bed so she could replay it all the next day.

After a couple of weeks, she began to wonder why. What was the purpose of it all? She could find another job, but nothing else would change—she'd go to work, go home to an empty house, prepare dinner, and start all over again the next day.

Where's the joy in that? she thought.

Maureen knew there had to be more, but she didn't know what she wanted. She'd already had the marriage, the family, the career … and look where that got her.

I have no idea what I want, so it's like I'm searching for the great unknown. How would I possibly know if I find it?

It was during one of her daily walks that she tucked into a coffee shop to find shelter from an unexpected rain shower. After ordering her usual, she walked to a table near the front window. On the way, she passed a community bulletin board that held business cards touting housecleaning services, dog walking, and landscaping. A flier was tacked to the board announcing a fundraiser for an injured firefighter. But what really caught her eye was a picture of a treasure chest and a QR code that simply said, "The journey of your lifetime starts here!"

What's that? she thought as she leaned in to get a closer look.

After setting down the hot cappuccino, she pulled out her phone and focused its camera on the QR code until it locked in on a website. Then she took her curiosity to the table to find out what it was all about.

"If someone handed you a map to life's greatest treasure, would you set sail on a voyage to discover the secrets within? Welcome to the journey of a lifetime, one that will take you to the treasure that is uniquely yours—a map that will guide you to the peace and joy that has been elusive for far too long.

A joyous tomorrow begins today. Register below to begin your life-changing journey."

Intrigued, Maureen read a little bit more about this Treasure Map to Joy™. At first, she was skeptical; after all, if she didn't know what would make her happy, how could someone else possibly know? But as she kept reading, she was pulled into the message. Perhaps the problem was even deeper—maybe she didn't even know what joy was, so she wouldn't recognize it, anyway.

Besides, she had to admit that the Treasure Map to Joy™ looked like it could be fun. Like a scavenger hunt or even the search for lost treasure in the show, The Curse of Oak Island, it seemed like a mysterious adventure, and the appeal grew on her. Before she talked herself out of it (like she'd been known to do in the past), she stepped out of her comfort zone and subscribed to learn more.

To her surprise, Leina replied the next morning. Introducing herself as a life coach, she welcomed her with a brief statement about the program. At the end, she pointed out that she had shared attachments to the email that would tell her more about the program.

As she devoured that material, Maureen learned that Leina offered two options: an online program and an in-person program that included one-on-one sessions, as well as group sessions where she'd meet other "treasure hunters." In the end, Maureen chose the in-person program.

If she was going on the treasure hunt of a lifetime, she wanted the full experience.

***

Maureen didn't know what to expect in her first meeting with Leina—after all, she'd never been on a treasure hunt before, and she'd never been on a quest for joy or happiness. Sure, she had felt both emotions from time to time, but they were always in conjunction with certain events—her wedding, the birth of her children, or a promotion. What others might call joy she called celebrations.

It had never occurred to her that joy could be a constant in her life—that is, until she met Leina. A petite woman, Leina had a big presence. There was something about her that radiated outward and touched Maureen on a deep level, and Maureen instantly felt drawn to how comfortable she was with herself and how genuine she was, as if Leina was right where she wanted to be at this moment in time.

When she asked Maureen what she was seeking from their work together, Maureen replied, "I want to be like you. I want to be content with my life and feel like I am right where I want to be. I do want some joy in my life, but right now, there just isn't any. And I don't even know where to begin to find it."

"Maureen, you've come to the right place. But let me tell you, I cannot give you all the answers you're looking for. And there's a good reason for that—what brings you joy is unique to you. While one person might be overjoyed when they're handed a playful puppy, another might be timid or even terrified. Different things bring joy to different people—and that's all good! That means your Treasure Map to Joy™ will be unique to you, and like a map of the world, it won't just lead you to a specific country, it will guide you right to the destination you desire," Leina explained.

"That would be amazing. Can you tell me how it works?" Maureen asked.

"For starters, I want you to think of this as a journey—a process." Leina said gently. "Each step along the way will reveal something new—about you, about what brings you joy, about what matters most. Every insight you uncover becomes a clue that leads to the next one. Before long, those pieces begin to form a map that's uniquely yours." Leina smiled and gestured toward a map on the wall. "Your *Treasure Map to Joy*™ will look different from anyone else's," she said. "It's not about chasing happiness or checking boxes. It's about uncovering what truly matters to you and learning how to live from that place."

She paused for a moment, letting her words settle. "Along the way, we'll explore the areas of your life that shape your overall sense of fulfillment. You'll start to see how they connect—how one affects the other—and how balance begins to form when you bring awareness to all of them."

Maureen nodded slowly. "Wow. That seems like a lot to work on, but I can tell you that I already see some areas where I have been neglecting myself. Like playfulness and self-care. And I have to admit that I haven't felt much gratitude lately. Maybe I've been focused on everything that's gone wrong," Maureen admitted.

"That's understandable," Leina replied. "But this process will help you rediscover the pieces that have been missing. Think of it as bringing light to what's been hidden. It's not about fixing yourself; it's about remembering what's already there. Joy isn't something you 'work on.' It's something you rediscover — through curiosity, awareness, and small, right actions. Each one reveals a little more of who you really are."

Leina continued with a slight smile "Approach this with a sense of wonder, like a child, excited about what it reveals and where it will take you. I think you'll find that the journey is just as rewarding and valuable as the destination."

"I'm actually getting excited!" Maureen stated. "So how do we start?"

"Before our next session," Leina said, "I want you to notice how joy is showing up in your life today. What's already bringing you joy? Where do you sense it's missing? Be conscious of it as you move through your days. If it helps, keep a small journal or jot notes in your phone — just enough to remind yourself of what you see and feel. The goal isn't to analyze; it's simply to become aware."

Maureen nodded, thinking it over. "I can do that," she said softly. "I'm not sure I'm feeling much joy lately like I said… but it sounds like an interesting experiment."

"Good," Leina said, smiling. "Let's set our next session."

They picked a time. As Maureen stood to leave, Leina reached for a folder on her desk. "One more thing before you go…"

3

At the end of their meeting, Leina handed Maureen a chart depicting her key life domains. She explained that these are the areas of life that, together, shape our overall wellbeing and happiness.

She then gazed into Maureen's eyes and said softly "When you don't know what to pursue in life, pursue yourself, and that's what we're going to do in this first module, the Life Assessment."

Maureen studied the page. "So, this is where I begin?"

Leina smiled. "Exactly. Before you can move toward joy and begin designing your future, you have to understand where you are today."

She then explained "In addition to noticing where joy shows up for you, I want you to log into your online program and complete the Life Assessment. You'll begin by ranking where you feel you are right now in each of those domains. Then you'll dig in a bit deeper to understand what's contributing to your rankings."

At first, Maureen was eager to dive in. Later that evening, curled up on her sofa with the chart in front of her, she assumed it would be fairly quick — just a few minutes to assign numbers to each area of her life.

But as she began, she realized it wasn't that simple. Ranking things was easy; reflecting on *why* she chose those rankings was not. The questions beneath each domain made her pause and think more deeply about her choices, her habits, and how she'd really been living.

Leina had mentioned that this exercise might bring up unexpected emotions and insights — that it was meant to stir awareness, not judgment. And now Maureen understood what she meant. This wasn't about filling in blanks; it was about facing herself.

The more she looked, the more she saw. Her relationships, her health, her work, even her sense of purpose — all of it seemed to connect. What began as a simple task quickly became something else entirely: a mirror.

She started with what felt easiest: her physical environment. "Okay, here we go!" she said out loud to herself.

***

Physical Environment: This one is easy, Maureen thought as she looked around her "home." There was nothing "homey" about it. There were no personal touches, with the exception of a few photographs of her children. She didn't feel warmth or excitement when walking through the door; nothing that really made a house a home. Still, it was clean and well maintained and in a good neighborhood, and it gave her shelter and security … for that, she was grateful. So, she gave it a "4," feeling her environment could be better, but knowing it could be worse.

Career: Initially, she swayed toward ranking her former job — that is until she remembered that this was all about how she felt today. And today, well, she didn't have a career. Yet, she did take a moment to think about how satisfied she'd been with her career before losing her job, and she was surprised that the job she had thought meant so much to her really didn't satisfy her at a deep level. It paid the bills, sure, but outside of monetary rewards, there were few. She scored it a 5.

Money and Finances: This domain was easier for Maureen. While she didn't have a current income, which she knew would impact her, she had lived frugally since the divorce. After their house was sold and the assets split evenly, she had put the money in savings and made a few small investments. It wasn't enough for her to retire on and live comfortably for the rest of her life, but she was grateful that she had made wise financial decisions. A lot of people who lost their jobs were in a much worse financial situation, so she ranked this domain a 5 too.

Health and Wellness: Maureen hesitated before assigning this one a score. Physically, she was fine — no major health issues, and she did her best to eat well. But emotionally? Mentally? That was harder to gauge. She'd been through so many changes lately that even the good days felt a little hollow. She realized she couldn't remember the last time she did something purely to care for herself. Something that really brought her joy. She went for walks sometimes and had gone to the movies alone last week, but even that had felt more like just passing time than living life. She gave this one a 5 realizing that she needed to do more to care for herself.

Family: Oh, Maureen loved her children, and she wouldn't trade them for anything in the world! They were a 10 in her book — but if she was being truthful with herself, she missed them after they'd left the nest. While she was proud of them, she wished they lived closer and were a bigger part of her everyday life. Text messages and 15-minute phone calls were okay, but they weren't a substitute for spending time together … and the laughter and hugs that she used to take for granted. She rated this area of her life a 7.

Significant Other / Romance: The divorce had hurt her deeply, and she had written off any idea of going down that path again. This was a 0 … and that didn't bother her. She just wasn't ready to get back into the dating game and didn't know if she ever would be.

Personal Growth: Maureen had always been a fan of *professional* growth, but she had neglected her *personal* growth. Still, she had to give herself some credit … after all, she was sitting here ranking the areas of her life, and she'd reached out to Leina for help. Knowing that was outside her norm, there was something to be said for that, and a small smile touched her lips as she changed her answer from a 0 to a 3.

Spirituality: Now, this was one area where Maureen was confident. She believed in a higher power and belonged to a church. When the kids were small, she insisted that they attend every week. She believed in being married in the eyes of God — one reason why she couldn't make peace with her marriage ending. When she ranked this area a 7, she made an internal promise to regularly attend their church once again … and wondered why her attendance had become sporadic.

Friends: While she admittedly didn't have many close friends, Maureen had one friend from childhood who had always been an important part of her life. While Robin had moved across the country when her husband had received a promotion, the two could go weeks without talking, but it was like no time had passed when they called each other again. Truth be told, Maureen didn't need or want a lot of friends — but she didn't want to think about where she would be without her dear Robin, who had been her lifeline when she was at her lowest. If there was one thing she would change about their relationship, though, it was that they'd see each other more often. She gave this one a 7 as she realized it might be nice to have friends closer to where she lived that could be part of her daily life.

Fun and Recreation: Hmm, well, I did go to the movies last week. Sure, I was alone, but it was something, she thought, as her finger hung over the keyboard before finally hitting the number 1.

After reviewing her responses one last time, Maureen hit "send" to submit her responses.

I might be a lost cause, she thought. *Leina might be in for more than she thought with me.*

***

Throughout the week, Maureen continued her job search, hoping that today would be the day that she'd get an email or call asking for an interview for the "perfect job." But in the back of her mind, she was beginning to wonder just what the perfect job looked like. What would it take for a job to truly bring her joy?

With that thought came the reminder that Leina had asked her to consider and write down the ways joy showed up in her life. True to her word, she had gone to church, and she welcomed the comfort and peace that it brought her. To her, that was joy, and she wrote it down, reminding herself once again to make sure this became a regular habit.

Outside of church, she remembered how excited she'd been when her daughter called her on a random Tuesday afternoon—for no reason other than to talk, she said, though she did have a few questions and wanted a recipe. Just seeing her daughter's name on the screen where her phone rang had brought an immediate smile to her face, and to Marueen, that was joy by itself.

And to her surprise, she found that she was actually looking forward to going through the online modules in Leila's program. She found that she was really enjoying the self-discovery that these initial tasks had brought and had gained a newfound sense of curiosity about where it could take her. It already had her thinking about how she could boost the rankings in her life domains, and rather than being negative or hesitant, she was ready to open that door and take the first step.

That is precisely what she asked Leila in their next session.

"Leila, there are so many low rankings in my life domains that I originally felt like a hopeless cause. I mean, there is sooo much missing, so much work to do. Yet, I'm hanging onto hope that you can help me, because, frankly, I'm not even sure where to start. I can tell you it's not going to be with romance, that's for sure. If this tells us where I'm at *right now* on my journey, what area do we even begin to tackle?" she asked.

"Maureen, from here on out, we're going to get introspective. It's not about simply assigning a rank—you've already done that. Oh no, we're going to go well beyond that and do a deep dive into each area to really gain an understanding of what is currently going on in each area of your life. While you may prefer to focus on one area, let me assure you that they each affect the others, particularly if one or more areas are out of alignment. For instance, with some people, we find that by focusing solely on their career, they jeopardize their personal relationships. As I look at your responses, I can see one thing right away is affecting multiple domains in your life," Leila gently said.

"Really?" Maureen eagerly replied. "And that would be…?"

"Connection," Leina replied gently. "Or maybe the absence of it. It shows up in different ways—in your relationships, in how little time you spend doing things that make you feel alive, even in how you take care of yourself. You've been through a lot, and it makes sense that you've pulled inward. But maybe that's where we begin—by finding small ways to reconnect, even if it's just with yourself at first."

Maureen nodded slowly, considering that. "You mean instead of just passing the time… actually *filling* it with something that feeds me?"

Leina smiled. "Exactly. Let's start there."

4

Immediately after submitting her completed assessment, Maureen wished she hadn't. She'd answered every question, but now the depth of what she'd written unsettled her. Some answers had come easily; others had stopped her cold, so she wrote something down just to move past it.

These questions asked her about her life as it was right now. They asked her to look closely at how she'd been living: what parts of her felt aligned and what parts were running on autopilot. They made her consider how her emotions shaped her choices, what beliefs she'd been carrying without question, whether her daily routines reflected her true values or just habit, and how *she* contributed to her score. Wow. That's not something she had really considered.

By the time she reached the end, Maureen realized this wasn't a quiz or a checklist—it was a mirror. And what it reflected back was a life that currently felt strangely hollow. That realization left her uneasy.

Frustrated, she found the need to clear her head, and the sun streaming through the window beckoned her to go outside. Maybe a walk would let it all sink in, help her clear her head, and quiet the noise her thoughts had stirred up.

Taking a deep breath of the late spring air, she immediately felt refreshed. For the first time in a long time, she walked with no purpose—there were no errands to run or places she needed to go. This was just a nice leisurely stroll through the neighborhood that she really hadn't bothered to get to know.

Fifteen minutes later, she entered the older part of the neighborhood. Its cobblestone walkways were lined with small shops and buildings that had been rejuvenated into boutiques and cafes, with trendy storefronts that attracted the attention of young couples and mothers pushing strollers. The entire block had been designed to appeal to this generation, and special care had been taken to make everything look picturesque, even the large displays of flowers and greenery that had been planted at regular intervals between the outdoor benches and dining areas.

One particular arrangement caught her eye. Already in full bloom, it was abundant with unusual coral and bright pink flowers, surrounded by lime green vines that spilled over its sides. Grabbing her phone, she took a picture, thinking she might be able to mimic the arrangement on a smaller scale on the small patio that to date had always been bare.

The renovated area ended at the end of the block, and as she entered the next, she encountered a different atmosphere—the cobblestone walkways were uneven, and the buildings told a different tale—one of weariness, even neglect. The buildings were old and had seen better days, but as she compared them with the newer storefronts she'd just passed through, it occurred to her that they had more character. The untouched architecture, weathered and worn, couldn't be replicated by modern construction, and she found herself hoping it never would be.

These buildings have history — they have value ... but it looks like they no longer have a purpose, she thought. *Kind of like me.*

The correlation hit her like a ton of bricks, and she suddenly wanted to capture the untold story, so she pulled out her phone, clicking pictures here and there until she had documented the entire block.

And when she returned home, it wasn't the bright and cheery flowers that called to her. No, she was drawn to the gray corbels, old wooden doors, and the cardboard signs that hung in the windows. What surprised her the most, though, was what she saw in the backgrounds of the photographs that she hadn't seen when she snapped them. It was the random person leaning against the side of an abandoned house, a dog resting on a step, a young mother pushing a stroller past a storefront window, and a beam of sunlight streaming from the sky on a cloudy day. To her, their appearance in an otherwise abandoned, neglected setting represented hope and life. It was like the past and what had been was merging with the present and what could be.

In the end, she still felt some frustration. But her outing had encouraged her not to give up. If those buildings still had a chance, so did she. So, even though she had toyed with the idea of canceling her next meeting with Leina, Maureen decided to go. She wanted to be upfront with Leina and express her doubts and feelings.

After listening patiently to Maureen's frustrations, Leina surprised her by telling her that she wasn't alone. As a matter of fact, Leina claimed that frustration was actually common at the beginning of the process.

"Most people aren't comfortable with being introspective, Maureen," she said. "And that's okay. My role is to help you gain that awareness. Actually, that's the first step in the process. So, you're right where you need to be."

"I just don't know where to go from here. It seems so overwhelming," Maureen admitted.

Leina nodded. "That's completely normal. Treasure doesn't always come easily, Maureen — sometimes we have to dig for it. The Assessment is part of that digging. It asks you to take a good, hard look at your life — not to judge it, but to understand it. That's where the clarity begins."

She paused before continuing. "It's not easy work. It stirs things up, and yes, it can bring a lot of emotion to the surface. But think about this — if you did nothing, if you just kept living as you are right now, where would you be in two years? Would you be any happier?"

Maureen thought for a moment, her eyes falling to the floor.

"Right now," Leina said softly, "you're a bit like someone in hibernation. And that's okay — it's a protective space. But awareness is what wakes us up. It's what brings life and color back into the picture."

Maureen sighed. "I'm not sure I can even answer the Assessment honestly, Leina. I might be a lost cause."

Leina smiled, shaking her head gently. "You're not a lost cause. You've already started by being honest about how you feel. Don't make this harder than it needs to be. The Assessment isn't about having perfect answers — it's about noticing what's there. Just let your truth show up on the page, even if it's messy or incomplete."

"That sounds… possible," Maureen said quietly.

"Exactly," Leina replied. "Awareness is the first step toward change. You don't have to have it all figured out — just stay curious. That's where transformation begins."

At the end of their meeting, Maureen agreed to continue with the Elevate Your Life® program — but this time, she did so with a little less fear and a little more curiosity.

***

The walk she'd taken had spurred more walks — it was something to do to pass the time, and it helped clear the turmoil and underlying sadness that consumed her days. When she set out the next Sunday morning, she grabbed her camera from her closet. It was an afterthought, and she'd almost forgotten she owned it.

Dusting it off, she wondered when she had used it last. Realizing that it was at her son's graduation, she smiled when she recalled that day. He looked so proud in his cap and gown, and she was even prouder. It had been a milestone to celebrate, and she'd gone all out, planning and hosting a party for their friends and family members. As she looked back, she realized she missed those days — days when she had a purpose.

Strange, when I was so busy being a wife and mother, I used to long for 'me' time. Now that I have it, I have no idea who I even am or what I even want to do with that time.

It was those thoughts that accompanied her on her walk, this time, to another neighborhood — again, a neglected, run down part of town. She didn't even realize that was where she was going until she found herself snapping pictures of a small church that sat next to a homeless shelter.

Snap. Snap. Snap.

As she moved to get a different vantage point, she noticed a man sitting on the ground, leaning against the church. And for the first time, she actually felt curious, wanting to know his story. Perhaps, he, too, had no family around, maybe he'd lost his job and had nowhere to go.

Suddenly, it occurred to her that her life, while far from joyful, wasn't all bad. After all, she did have a roof over her head. It might not be the dream house that they'd designed and built, but it was a place to call home.

With that thought, she reached into her pocket and pulled out a $10 bill. Although he appeared to be sleeping, she cautiously approached him, attempting not to startle him too much. Hearing her footsteps, he opened his eyes, and she handed him the money.

"Here," she said. "In case you're hungry."

The man stared at her for a moment, and she could see the uncertainty in his eyes before he reached out and took the money.

"Thank you. Do you work here?" he asked, nodding toward the shelter.

"Me? Oh, no. I was just passing through. Actually, I was taking some pictures of the church. It really is quite quaint," she explained.

It was a brief interaction, and one that wouldn't usually stick with her. She'd seen homeless people before and had given them money before. But this time, something was different. She wondered if he also questioned whether *he* mattered. Did he long for more, like she did, but have no idea what that looked like?

As she continued to walk, though, her world felt just a little lighter. For the first time in a long time, she felt that today she had made a difference in someone else's life. To Maureen, that felt good.

When she returned to her apartment, she even pulled up her life assessment once again. Maybe this time, things would look a little clearer.

When she was done with her additions, she jotted a note to Leina, saying that she was working on it and thought she was making some progress.

Then, she mentioned that she'd gained a different perspective, in part, after meeting the homeless man.

"It made me feel good to know that I could help him, even if it wasn't much," she said.

When Leina read the message, she realized that Maureen was actually making headway. She made a note in Maureen's profile:

"Maureen needs to be needed. She just doesn't know how meaningful that is to her yet."

A small smile touched her lips when she added, "But she will."

5

Maureen was Leina's last appointment of day, and while Leina was looking forward to the weekend, she was excited to hear from her new client. She found she really liked Maureen, and she really wanted to see where her treasure map would take her. Would it lead her to a new career, perhaps a renewed relationship with her children? It was too soon to tell, but Leina was confident that Maureen was on a path of discovery that would change her life for the better.

She has so much to offer and has been such a good mother, employee, and member of society. It will be interesting to watch her transformation and see who Maureen really becomes when she focuses on her needs and wishes after spending so many years caring for everyone else, she thought.

When Maureen walked through the door at 4:00 sharp, Leina took that as a sign that Maureen was excited as well.

"It's good to see you! I've been looking forward to our meeting since you contacted me. It sounds like you've had a good week," Leina said.

"I did. I'm finding that I'm enjoying playing around with photography again. It's been so long that I forgot how much I liked taking pictures back when the kids were younger. But this time around, I'm a bit surprised that I'm seeing things differently. It's not about setting up the best shot, if you will, but about documenting things that I once turned a blind eye to … things that I never noticed before," Maureen shared.

"Perhaps your perspective has changed over the years," Leina said thoughtfully. "That's what this process is all about — seeing your life with new eyes. Tell me, what did you notice as you went through the assessment again?"

Maureen exhaled softly. "More than I expected, honestly. At first, it felt like work — like filling out forms. But as I went deeper, it made me think about how much of my life I've just been moving through on autopilot. Some of the questions really got under my skin."

Leina smiled. "That's usually a sign you're asking the right questions."

"I guess so," Maureen said. "It wasn't easy to look at the areas where I've been stuck, or how much of myself I've lost over the years. There were moments I wanted to skip entire sections, especially when it asked about what emotions I associate with each part of my life. That's where it hit me — how disconnected I've been."

Leina nodded, listening closely. "It takes courage to see that clearly. When we start shining light on parts of life we've avoided, it stirs things up. But that discomfort means you're no longer ignoring it—you're aware of it. And awareness is the first real step toward change."

"That's what I'm starting to realize," Maureen admitted. "When I looked across everything, I noticed a pattern—this feeling of emptiness or isolation like you mentioned in our last session, even in areas that I thought were okay. I used to think it was just about losing my marriage, but it's more than that."

Leina leaned forward slightly. "What do you think it's about?"

Maureen paused, her gaze distant. "You know, I don't think it started when my kids grew up or when my marriage ended. Even before all that—when life was busy and things were just humming along—I see now how much of it carried its own momentum. The kids were in school, I had work, there were activities, dinners, errands, plans. I kept up with it all, but I wasn't really *steering* any of it. Life was moving, but I wasn't the one directing where it was going."

She took a breath, her voice softening. "I think I mistook that constant movement for purpose. It kept me occupied, but I wasn't always... alive in it. And when that momentum stopped—when the marriage ended and the kids grew up—it was like the current went still, and I didn't know how to move myself forward."

Leina nodded slowly, her tone both compassionate and steady. "That's such an important realization, Maureen. When the activities of our lives create the momentum of our lives, it can look like fulfillment—but it's really just motion. What you're describing is the difference between being carried by life and consciously choosing your direction. And the moment you start seeing that difference, you're already beginning to reclaim your power."

Maureen exhaled, a hint of emotion in her voice. "That makes so much sense. I don't know why I didn't see that before."

Leina smiled softly, letting the weight of Maureen's words settle. "What you've just realized isn't small, Maureen—it's a breakthrough. You've begun to see where life was carrying you instead of you guiding it with intention. Sit with that for a while. Let it unfold. This new awareness is powerful—it helps you see what you want to create moving forward. You're not starting over; you're applying everything you've learned, everything you've lived, to the next chapter of your life—only this time, with conscious choice behind it."

Maureen smiled faintly. "That sounds a lot kinder than starting over."

Leina's eyes softened. "It is. Growth rarely asks us to erase the past—it invites us to build on it with new understanding."

Maureen sat quietly, absorbing her words. For the first time, she could feel a faint but steady sense of clarity—like a light turning on in a room she hadn't realized was dark. She didn't need to overhaul her life; she just needed to start noticing it again.

Her gaze drifted toward the window, and she smiled faintly. "Like photography," she said. "When I'm behind the camera, I actually feel present. It's not about escaping—it's about noticing. And that's new for me."

Leina's eyes lit up. "That's exactly what I mean. You're reconnecting with a part of yourself that knows how to see beauty, how to be fully present, even in ordinary moments. Follow that. It's more than a hobby—it's a clue."

Maureen laughed gently. "A clue to what?"

"To yourself," Leina replied with a knowing smile. "The assessment showed you where things feel off-balance. Those insights—combined with what you're rediscovering through photography—are already shaping your next steps. You don't have to force direction; it's revealing itself."

Maureen nodded slowly, taking it in. "I guess it really is a process."

"It is," Leina agreed. "And you're right where you should be in it. Keep reflecting on what feels meaningful, what energizes you, and what no longer fits. That awareness will become the foundation for what comes next."

For the first time, Maureen felt the heaviness she'd been carrying begin to lift. "Thank you, Leina," she said quietly. "I don't know where this is leading yet—but for once, that feels okay."

Leina smiled. "That's the perfect place to begin."

***

By the next morning, Maureen had decided that she wanted to visit her son for his birthday. It was only two weeks away, and she hoped he would be as excited to see her as she was to see him.

Pulling out her phone, she sent him a text.

"Hi, just checking to see if you're free the week of your birthday. I've got plenty of time and would love to come see you!"

A few minutes later, he replied.

"Hey, Mom. I'd love to see you too, but I'm sorry, I'm going camping that week."

Trying not to let her disappointment show, Maureen tried to be lighthearted.

"Oh, that's nice. I hope you have a good time. Who are you camping with?"

His one-word response caused her heart to fall.

"Dad," he wrote.

With that, Maureen felt a surge of emotions as so many things went through her mind: it just wasn't fair — hadn't her ex-husband taken enough from her? Her home, her marriage, her life. Wasn't it enough that he had moved on without a care in the world? Did he have to rob her of time with her son, too?

As the anger and jealousy were slowly taken over by sadness, she couldn't bear the thought of being alone in her apartment a moment longer. Grabbing her keys and her purse, she headed out the door. At the last second, she turned back and grabbed her camera, hoping it would take her attention off everything that was wrong in her life.

6

As if on autopilot, Maureen's feet pounded the pavement. To onlookers, she appeared to be a woman on a mission, but in reality, she had no idea where she was going. In a way, she didn't care—her mind wasn't centered on where she wanted to go; instead, it was focused on the fact that her son was going camping with her ex-husband.

It's just not fair, she thought. *He tore our family apart! Now, he's selfishly claiming birthdays and holidays with our kids, leaving me with nothing.*

As all the old feelings and resentment returned, Maureen recognized what was happening. The familiar ache surprised her — she had honestly thought she'd moved past it. But here it was again, rising uninvited. The truth was, healing wasn't linear. Like Leina had once told her, sometimes life presents us with moments that reopen old wounds, not to set us back, but to invite a deeper level of healing. This was one of those moments, and Maureen could feel it.

She continued thinking about that and before long, her anger and jealousy began to subside, giving way to acceptance and understanding.

It is what it is, she thought. *And like I've told my kids, the divorce wasn't their fault.*

Then she had an eye-opening thought:

Why am I upset that they still have a relationship with their father? I can remember a time when I would have been happy for them to go camping and spend time together. I would've even encouraged it and packed their bags!

That thought brought forth an unexpected smile. Oh, back in the day, she would have definitely welcomed them spending some bonding time together.

And now that they were doing precisely what she had always wanted, she was finding fault with it and allowing it to eat at her happiness. The irony wasn't lost on her. When she thought about it, she actually *wanted* them to have a relationship with their father, yet here she was, upset about it. *Oh Maureen. Life is funny — not funny.*

As she mulled these thoughts, Maureen pulled out her camera. Without thinking, she started snapping pictures — a faded storefront, a young couple holding hands, the steeple of an old stone church — the same church she had photographed the week before.

Looking toward the church, she wondered if she'd see the same man again, the one she gave money to, but he wasn't in sight. The shelter next door, though, seemed to be livelier than the first time she passed. Its doors were propped open, and on impulse, she decided to step inside.

"Hi, are you the new volunteer?" a woman asked, flashing a friendly smile.

"Me? Oh, no … I was just walking by and decided to walk in. I'm sorry, I guess I shouldn't have," Maureen answered.

"Don't be sorry. We welcome everyone. You're free to stay. Let me know if you have any questions. I'd give you a tour, but frankly we're preparing lunch right now, and things usually start to get a little hectic. There's just so much to do — that's why I was hoping you were our new volunteer. We could use a few extra hands, for sure," she said.

"I bet," Maureen replied. "How many people do you feed?"

"Sometimes 70, sometimes 100 or more. I've tried to keep track so I could study the trends and have a better estimate, but again, who has the time? Not me!"

"Hmmm, you know, I do have experience with projections and estimates. Maybe I could help?" Maureen suggested, surprising even herself.

"That would be amazing, especially since it's not one of my strengths. By the way, my name is Joanne, but everyone calls me Jo," she said. "I run the kitchen at the shelter," she said.

"I'm Maureen, and while I'm not the volunteer you were looking for, I have some free time. Can I help?"

"You bet you can! Go through those doors to the kitchen and ask José for an apron. You can't miss him — he's a big guy — affectionately known as Moose. Tell him I sent you and that you're going to help serve today. He'll tell you what to do," Jo said, as she flung a tea towel over her shoulders. "Now, I've got to get busy; otherwise, we're going to have a lot of hungry people without lunch!"

Two hours later, Maureen had carried the last of the macaroni and cheese pans into the kitchen and wiped down all of the tables when she ran into Jo again.

"How'd it go?" she asked.

"Okay, I think I'll get the hang of it better next time," she admitted.

"So, you're coming back?" Jo asked.

"Yes, I think so. Is there a schedule or something?"

"We're here every day Monday through Friday. There's a sign-up sheet on the bulletin board by the office. You can pick any days you want," Jo directed.

Five minutes later, Maureen had signed up to volunteer three days that week. And although she was tired, she left with a bounce in her step.

"It felt really good to help," she texted Leina. "And I'm already thinking about how they can project how many people will walk through the door a little better, so they can plan and be more efficient. I was really down, but the experience shifted my attitude a lot."

The text was just the invitation Leina needed to touch base with Maureen about her progress in the program. Earlier that morning, she'd sent Maureen the next module — Aspirations — the part of the journey where awareness begins to turn into vision.

"That sounds wonderful, Maureen," she wrote. "As you move into the Aspirations Module, which I sent you this morning, you'll start exploring what you truly want to experience next — what feels meaningful and alive for you. I think you'll begin to notice even more of a shift.

You know, your experience reminds me that so many of us focus our thoughts on what we think is wrong in our lives and on our shortcomings. We forget that we all have strengths and characteristics that can bring real value— to ourselves and to the people around us. Before we meet again, I'd like you to take a strengths assessment to discover yours. It's simple, insightful, and honestly, kind of fun. I think you'll find it really useful—I know I did!"

Curling her legs up on the sofa, Maureen hesitantly clicked the link Leina had included in the email. The Assessment had been tough—emotionally draining, even—so she hoped this next part might feel a little lighter. Maybe, just maybe, Aspirations would help her glimpse where to go from here. She had nothing to lose but time—and she had plenty of that.

7

"You were right, Leina, the strengths assessment didn't take long, and it was easy!" Maureen said.

"And I have found that it's quite accurate — I know mine was," Leina stated. Too often, we are so focused on what we believe are our shortcomings that we forget we have something of real value to offer. The results are relevant in so many things you'll do, from defining a career path to creating meaningful relationships, even discovering your unique path to happiness."

"Hmmm, well, leadership appears to be one of my strengths, but I never actually saw myself as a leader," Maureen admitted.

"I disagree," Leina piped in. "For two decades, you ran a household and a family, and you did quite a commendable job. And didn't you say you were a team leader in your most recent job? It looks to me like leadership has been apparent in many areas of your life."

"I guess I hadn't thought of it that way. The strengths assessment also mentioned creativity and humanity. It did point out that bravery or courage is not my strong trait," Maureen added.

"We are going to take all of that into account as we create your Treasure Map to Joy™. Using your strengths to your advantage will make the journey a little easier," Leina explained.

"Now, the purpose of Module Two is to start exploring your Aspirations—what you truly want in life," Leina explained. "But I'm not talking about external goals as much as I am about how you want your life to *feel*.

Let's say you want to find a new job—great! But we'll go deeper than that. How do you want to feel in that job? Fulfilled? Valued? Inspired?

Or maybe you want to make changes in your home. That's wonderful too, but we'll look at how you want to feel *when you're there*. Peaceful? Grounded? Joyful?

Does that make sense?"

"Yes, it does, but one of my problems is that I don't know what I want my life to look like. I just…don't know. But what I *do* know is that I don't want to keep living on autopilot. I'm ready for more than just getting through the day. I just don't know what that future looks like anymore. I used to—once."

Leina smiled gently. "That's okay, Maureen. Remember, your life isn't a problem to solve—it's a journey to embrace. Every experience you've had has shaped your wisdom, and now it's about using that wisdom to chart your own Treasure Map to Joy™.

Just like the seasons change, so do we. What worked in one season of your life may not fit in the next—and that's not failure, it's growth. You're simply in a new season now.

We're not here to dwell on the past; we're here to honor it while designing a future that feels meaningful and alive. And if you're not sure yet what you *do* want, start with what you know you don't. That's where clarity begins."

Then Leina leaned forward, her tone both gentle and curious. "Let's try something for a moment. Close your eyes and fast forward two years. If nothing changes—if you keep living exactly as you are now—what does that look like for you?"

Maureen did as she asked. Her shoulders sank slightly, and a heaviness crossed her face. The vision felt too familiar—days blending together, the same routines, the same emptiness.

"Now," Leina continued softly, "imagine instead that something *has* changed. That you've been intentional, even in small ways. What would your days feel like then? What would you be doing differently? Who would you be becoming?"

Maureen's expression shifted, her brow easing. She pictured herself waking up with a sense of purpose, laughing more, maybe working again—doing something meaningful. She imagined dinners with her kids, feeling connected instead of distant. The images were hazy but hopeful, and she realized how much she missed that feeling.

Leina smiled as Maureen slowly opened her eyes, emotion flickering there.

"I keep trying to think about who I was… but who am I now? Am I the reason nothing is changing?"

"That's a powerful question, Maureen," Leina said gently. "And it's not about blame—it's about awareness. Change doesn't start by fixing everything at once; it starts by noticing. You're already doing that." She paused. "If this feels uncomfortable, that's okay. It means something inside you is waking up. Discomfort isn't a stop sign—it's a sign you're stretching."

Maureen hesitated, then exhaled. "But what if I pick the wrong things for my aspirations, and it leads me down a path where I won't be happy? What if I think I want something, but it's not really what I want? I used to be able to dream, Leina. Now I don't even know what I'd dream about."

"Maureen," Leina said softly, "maybe you're waiting for permission—to want something just for yourself. What if there is no 'wrong' choice right now? What if this stage isn't about finding the perfect path, but about rediscovering your curiosity? You're not designing the rest of your life—just the next version of it."

"Okay, I think I get it. I'll do my best, but I'm going to need your help, Leina. How do I get started?" Maureen asked.

"Start small," Leina encouraged. "You don't need all the answers today. When you begin working through the Aspirations module, let your attention go toward what sparks a little energy—something that feels alive, even in a subtle way. Sometimes clarity shows up *while* you're reflecting, not before. Let the process surprise you."

That felt manageable, Maureen thought. Still, she wasn't sure where to begin. But if there was one thing she could count on, it was her determination. When she committed to something, she followed through. Maybe this process would help her reconnect to something she hadn't felt in a while—hope.

***

Later that evening, Maureen curled up on the sofa with her laptop and opened the Aspirations module. The questions looked familiar, echoing the same life domains she'd explored before — but this time, the focus was different. Instead of *where am I now?* she was being asked, *what do I want this part of my life to look and feel like?*

She decided to start with her home. It seemed like the simplest place to begin — but her first thought stopped her cold: *I can't really change much here. I don't even own this house.* It wasn't like the home she and her husband had built together — the one that once felt so perfectly *theirs.*

Still, she wanted to try. Hoping to spark some inspiration, Maureen grabbed her keys and headed to a big-box home store, wandering through aisles of lamps, artwork, and accessories. Everything looked nice enough, but it all felt generic. Nothing felt *like her.*

Maybe it's not about buying new things, she thought as she drifted past a row of framed prints. *Maybe it's about bringing myself back into my space.* Then it hit her — *my photos.* She could develop them, frame them, make her walls reflect her own eyes again.

It wasn't much, but it was a start — and that small idea stirred something in her.

On the drive home, she noticed the way the late-afternoon light fell across the city, how the long shadows stretched across the sidewalk like quiet invitations. Her thoughts wandered — to her photos, to the shelter, to the easy conversations she'd shared with Jo and the other volunteers. The work gave shape to her days. It reminded her what it felt like to connect, to belong, to matter.

That's when it clicked. *Leina was right.* When you start taking action — even small ones — clarity begins to form. She hadn't planned any of this. She'd picked up her camera on a whim, walked into the shelter without expectation, and yet here she was, feeling something real again. Maybe this was what forward motion looked like—simple steps that quietly start changing everything.

For the first time in a long while, she realized she *did* know some things about what she wanted. She wanted more of this—more meaning, more connection, more life that felt real.

Later that evening, she opened her laptop and looked at the Aspirations module again. Maybe she didn't have every answer, but she could start here—with what made her feel alive. She smiled, realizing she'd even stopped scrolling through job listings. For now, finding herself felt more important than finding another position. Maybe once she understood what she truly wanted, the rest would sort itself out.

***

A few days later, Leina's words echoed in her mind: *If there's something important you want, take action—any action—to make it happen. No one can do that for you.*

Maureen had been thinking a lot about her children. They were grown, living their own lives, and she'd told herself they were too busy to stay in touch. But maybe she'd been waiting for them to reach out—when it was really up to her.

That night, she opened her phone and typed a quick message: *Hey, can we set up a Zoom this weekend? I'd love to see you both.*

8

How was your weekend?" Jo asked Maureen when she walked into the shelter Monday morning.

"Noneventful, for the most part," Maureen answered. "I did a little shopping and spent some time rearranging furniture."

"Oh, expecting company, are you?"

"No, just ready for a change, I guess. I'm not really sure what I'm going to do with my living room, but I hope it will come to me. My daughter, who is a minimalist, says I just need to find one focal piece, and I'll be good. But that sounds a bit stark to me, and that's what I'm trying to get away from. Our old house was warm—it felt like *home*," Maureen shared as she opened a gallon-sized can of baked beans.

"Don't forget to add extra brown sugar to those," Jo instructed.

"Will do," Maureen smiled.

"So, where was this 'home' that you speak of—your old home?" Jo asked as she added another pan of grilled chicken patties to the 18-quart roaster.

"In Rivers Edge. Have you heard of it?"

Letting out a small whistle, Jo replied, "Sure have. Nice area, Maureen. So, how'd you end up here?"

"Divorce," Maureen sighed. "I guess I wanted to put some distance between myself and the past, so I moved to this side of town, where I'm not likely to run into my ex. I came across this food kitchen by chance while exploring. How did you wind up working here, Jo?"

"Well, I love to cook, and some say I'm pretty good at it. When I heard about the job opening, I was a line cook at a diner and thought it would be an opportunity for me to serve the community while doing what I love. So, I applied."

"I thought you were a volunteer, like me," Maureen replied.

"I'm an employee. I manage this kitchen, and Luis manages the one on the east side of town," explained Jo.

"There's another one?"

"Yes, and there's an overnight shelter, too," she shared.

"Who pays you?" Maureen asked.

"The Foundation. We're actually a not-for-profit, and the funds come from grants, the government, and then, of course, donations from businesses and the community. Like tomorrow—on the first Tuesday of the month, Mario's Pizza donates pizzas to our kitchen, and we just have to provide salad and a dessert. It works out great because it gives me an opportunity to visit the other kitchen and do some shopping. And I have to stop by the shelter, as well, to drop off last month's numbers so Mark, our director, can submit his monthly report for the grant."

"I'm usually not here on Tuesdays, but if you need extra help, I can stop by," Maureen volunteered.

"Thanks, but I think we'll be okay. As a matter of fact, I just have to ice these cakes, and everything will be ready for the volunteers to serve. If you want to frost one of them, that'd be great," Jo suggested. "Just flip the cake onto that cake platter, and we'll be done in no time."

"Oh, Jo, I might not be the best person for that job. I've never been able to flip a cake out of the pan without making a mess of it. It cracks every time," admitted Maureen.

"Here's the trick. Don't flip the cake onto the platter. Instead, place the platter over the cake and then flip it upside down," said Jo.

Holding her breath and praying that she wouldn't destroy the cake too much, Maureen followed instructions.

"Here goes nothing," she said as she gently lifted the pan.

"Ta-da! I did it, Jo! I think it's the first time I haven't made a mess trying to put a cake on a serving platter!"

"It's perfect. We'll be out of here in no time," Jo said.

***

That evening, Maureen was feeling pretty good. She really enjoyed talking and working with Jo, and even though it was a little thing, she was still pretty proud of herself for successfully getting a cake out of a pan without making a mess of it.

On top of that, she was happy with the call she had with her kids. At the beginning, it was a little stilted, especially when Maureen brought up the camping trip her son had taken with his father. When she sensed his reluctance to talk about it, she quickly switched the subject and told them that she'd turned the extra bedroom into a darkroom and had been developing a few of the pictures she'd taken. To her surprise, her kids actually sounded interested.

"That's great, Mom!" Sophie exclaimed. "You always took the best pictures. Remember all of the pictures you took of me in my dance recitals? My friends used to think you were a professional photographer, and I let them because it made me feel cool."

"Good for you, Soph," Jake interjected. "But it wasn't so easy for me."

"How so?" Maureen asked, curious.

"Well, how about the time you took a picture of my room and said you were going to submit it to the high school yearbook committee so I could be voted to be 'Most Likely to be the World's Messiest Bachelor?'"

Like old times, the three erupted in laughter, adding to the humor.

"But it worked, Jake. It got you to clean that pigsty of a room!" Maureen added.

"Well, that and the fact that you also threatened to take away my Nintendo if I didn't get it done," he sheepishly admitted. "On another note, you'll be pleased to know that I'm better now. I actually got my laundry done this morning, *and* I put it all away. I had to get it done before the game starts this afternoon."

"Still a Cubs fan?" she asked.

"Once a Cubs fan, always a Cubs fan," he laughed.

From there, Sophie asked a few questions about the type of pictures Maureen had been taking. When Maureen told them that she was going to make a gallery wall in her living room, her daughter interjected, stating that she thought one large picture would look better. "I'm a minimalist, Mom, remember? Less is sometimes more."

"I'm still trying to figure out what I am, Soph, but I'll keep that in mind. Who knows? Maybe I can incorporate both into the living room," Maureen stated.

In the end, Jake said he was sorry but the game was starting soon… "You know how it is." As they tookhe call, Sophie surprised her mother.

"Hey, Mom…"

"Yes?" Maureen waited, sensing her daughter's hesitation.

"I just wanted to say that I enjoyed our talk today."

Smiling, Maureen replied, "I did, too. I really did."

"Me, too," Jake added. "Now, I gotta go! Bye."

That was it. They steered clear of conversation about the divorce and somehow avoided talking about anything of importance. It wasn't an emotional call, but it left Maureen feeling better about her relationship with her children than she had in a long time.

And that's when it occurred to her that maybe, just maybe, her children weren't comfortable talking to *her*. She quickly grabbed her journal and wrote down her thoughts.

Are my kids avoiding me because they don't know what to say or do to make me feel better?

Do they somehow feel that they're responsible for my happiness?

And then she added a couple noteworthy thoughts that she wanted to share with Leina:

It felt so good to talk and laugh with Jake and Sophie again, even if we played it safe.

When she returned home from volunteering, she added one more:

I'm still grinning! Who knew that something as small as taking a cake out of a pan could bring me joy … if that's what joy feels like.

***

When she talked with Leina about her experiences, Leina listened thoughtfully and offered some great insight.

"Maureen, joy isn't something you achieve—it's something you allow. You *can* be joyful when a cake you baked slides easily out of a pan! You can be joyful about anything!"

"But it seems like such a small thing," Maureen admitted.

"Maybe so," Leina said, smiling. "Those small things really do add up. And when it comes to your children, it's okay to talk about the past and share memories—it's part of how we stay connected. There might be some discomfort at first, and that's natural. Your role as a mother is changing, and that can feel like losing a piece of yourself. But their roles are changing too. They're learning how to show up as adults and to relate to you in new ways, just as you're learning how to show up in this season of your own life. It's not about going back—it's about finding new ways to meet each other where you are now."

Leina's reassuring words left Maureen feeling optimistic about the steps she was taking toward her Aspirations, and for the first time in a long time, she gave herself permission to be excited about where it would take her.

9

The optimism from her call with the kids carried into the following week. For the first time in a long time, Maureen felt like things were shifting—subtly, but genuinely. Leina had been right: if she wanted something to change, she had to take part in creating that change. Reaching out to her kids had proven it; that conversation never would have happened if she hadn't made the first move.

As the week went on, she found herself more at ease at the shelter. The faces that once felt unfamiliar were becoming part of her routine, and the laughter she shared with Jo and the other volunteers reminded her how good it felt to belong somewhere again. They joked easily while they worked, and she realized she looked forward to seeing them. When they invited her to join a weekend game of pickleball, she hesitated for only a moment before saying yes. She'd never played before, but she'd been good at tennis in high school—and besides, she was beginning to enjoy saying yes to new things.

Excitedly, she stopped by the store to buy herself a racquet. If she watched a couple videos, she thought she could get a good grasp of the game and not make a fool of herself.

Still, the thought didn't scare her. She actually found that she was looking forward to it.

Thankfully, when Saturday rolled around, she was happy to see that they were all amateurs. There were plenty of missed shots, including hers, but the game was filled with laughter and good-natured teasing. Maureen didn't feel intimidated or self-conscious at all. When they asked if she'd play again, she quickly replied, "Count me in!"

The optimism from her call with the kids lingered through the week, carrying her into the days that followed with a little more lightness. By the time the next Monday morning rolled around, she felt almost surprised to realize she was looking forward to what the week might bring.

That's when her phone rang.

Not recognizing the number, she hesitantly answered, only to find that it was a human resources department calling about a position she applied for weeks ago.

"Maureen, the position you applied for has been filled. But we do have another position available that we think you would be perfect for. While it's not a supervisory position, there is the possibility of advancement down the road," they explained.

Taking a few minutes to learn about the job and the pay, Maureen immediately knew she was overqualified. While it was a job, it was just a step above entry-level, and it would definitely be a step back, not a step forward, in her career.

"While we don't mean to rush you, Maureen," the woman said, "we would like an answer as soon as possible so we get our team in place."

Suddenly, something Leina had said popped into her head.

"It's about how you feel, Maureen. How do you want to *feel* in your home? How do you want to *feel* in a job?"

Before she knew it, the words flew out of her mouth.

"I'm sorry, I don't think I'm interested at this time," she said. "The position isn't what I'm looking for."

Feeling confident that she had just made a major decision in her life, Maureen hung up the phone and got ready for another day at the shelter.

Fifteen minutes later, she couldn't believe what she had just done.

What was I thinking? I want a job – I need a job! And that was a sure thing. It was mine, all I had to do was say the word. But no, not me, I seem to be hell bent on staying in a rut. I don't deserve joy in my life ... when the door opens, I slam it in my own face!

Kicking herself, she thought about picking up the phone and calling the company back to sincerely apologize and see if they would still consider her for the job.

But she didn't.

Instead, she chose to beat herself up a while longer, wondering why she kept sabotaging her own happiness.

"You okay?" Jo asked, noticing that Maureen had been unusually quiet during most of her shift.

"Uh, yeah. Yes, I am, thank you," Maureen answered, caught off guard as Jo's questions interrupted the second guessing going on in her head. "Just preoccupied, I guess."

"Okay," Jo replied, not fully believing her. "You know I'm here if you need anything."

"Thank you, Jo," Maureen responded, choosing to keep her thoughts to herself.

"Hey, Maureen, a change of pace might do you good. Do you want to come with me Tuesday? I have to do some shopping and want to stop by the other kitchen to talk to Luis. Oh, and we also need to swing by the overnight community shelter while we're out. Are you available? I could use the company."

"Sure, I think I'd like that," Maureen smiled.

Yet, the regret for turning down the job offered lingered, so much that she knew she had to reach out to Leina later that afternoon.

"I don't know what's wrong with me," she said, pacing as she talked. "Just as things start moving in the right direction, I do something that makes no sense. Who turns down a perfectly good job when they need one?"

Leina's voice was calm. "Maybe someone who's starting to listen to herself."

Maureen frowned. "What do you mean?"

"Well," Leina said, "you said it yourself—you imagined yourself in that job and didn't like the way it made you feel. That matters. Maybe your decision wasn't self-sabotage. Maybe it was self-awareness. Perhaps that job would have kept you stuck in the same patterns you've been trying to move beyond."

Maureen sighed. "But I turned down a job, Leina. That's huge. I'm single, I'm unemployed—it feels reckless."

"It feels uncomfortable," Leina corrected gently. "And discomfort can look a lot like recklessness when you're used to playing it safe. But think about it—you're standing at the edge of a bridge. You can cross toward what's next, or step back into what's familiar. That job might have been a step backward, and some part of you already knew that."

Maureen was quiet for a long moment. "But I still need a paycheck. Maybe I should've just taken it until something better came along."

"Your instincts told you otherwise," Leina said. "You're not rejecting work, you're redefining what kind of work fits the life you're building. You can honor the experiences that brought you here without repeating them. They've given you wisdom—but that doesn't mean you have to live them again. Every choice you make from here on out can be guided by what feels aligned, not just what feels safe."

Leina's words brought her some reassurance, but she knew she had suffered a setback as she found herself revisiting her decision again a few days later. At least, she had something to look forward to—spending Tuesday with Jo. That would be a welcome distraction.

And it was. They traveled across town and met Luis, an energetic and kind man who was devoted to the kitchen he ran. Maureen was impressed when she observed him interacting with their lunch guests, knowing most of them on a first-name basis.

"He really seems to like his job," Maureen pointed out.

"Oh, he does. Actually, he lives for it," Jo advised.

From there, they went to the overnight shelter, where she met with the director of the foundation. Mark was in his mid-60's and had held the position for the last ten years, he explained before pointing out that he would be retiring next spring.

"It's time for someone else to take over. I only intended to stay for five years, but time got away from me. It's now time for me and the wife to do some traveling and see the rest of the world," he explained.

A quick tour of the facilities showed Maureen that it was much like the shelter kitchens, with cinder block walls and linoleum floors. It lacked style or any personal touch whatsoever, even in the community room, which held a handful of tables and chairs and yet another bulletin board that posted the shelter's rules. The only personal items anywhere were a couple decks of cards and a game of checkers that rested on a table by the door.

Maureen was still thinking about the shelter being underutilized when they walked outside, and a bridge across the street caught her eye.

"What's that?" she asked Jo, pointing to an old wooden covered bridge.

"Oh, that's the old Sanders Bridge. It used to be the only way to get across the river. Okay, I guess it's more like a big creek. But anyway, when they put in the four-lane highway, they built the big steel bridge a couple miles up the road. This bridge has since been deemed to be an historic landmark, but as you can see from the signs, it's only open to foot traffic. No cars allowed," Jo explained.

"It's gorgeous," Maureen softly said as she stood at the opening. "I wonder what's on the other side."

"It'll take you to the old part of town—you know, houses that were once grand, but are now rundown and split into apartments. It's a shame—it used to be *the* place to live years ago, but shopping malls and the shift to suburban living changed that," Jo said.

As Maureen looked at the architecture of the structure, she couldn't help but remember what Leina had said. Like this bridge, she stood on one bank—ready to cross to the life on the other.

And she knew right where she wanted to go. She couldn't wait to get home to grab her camera so she could come back and take some pictures.

It was just what she had been looking for…

10

Click…Click. The afternoon sun pierced through the opening of the bridge, providing just enough light so she could see the entire length of the inside of the wooden structure.

Maureen knew she'd snapped dozens of pictures from every angle imaginable. However, she hadn't yet crossed the bridge. For now, she was fascinated with it from where she stood.

With no destination, she found herself walking down the street. She didn't even realize she was humming a tune until she passed someone else strolling by, and she caught herself.

Then it occurred to her that she was actually humming — did that mean she was happy?

She had to admit that it was starkly different than the day just a couple months before when she'd taken a walk and stumbled upon the shelter. There had been no humming that day. Instead, she recalled feeling out of place. She was all alone and in an unfamiliar area when she'd wandered around that day. She hadn't felt upbeat at all. If anything, she'd been in a fog—a thick fog that wouldn't lift so she could see beyond that moment, that day.

That's it, she thought. That's what's different! I'm no longer in a fog. I've stepped out of it now. I'm still unemployed, and I still miss my kids, but things have changed. With Leina's help, I've given myself permission to try something new. I'm volunteering and have made friends with Jo and the gang. I'm getting out of the house, taking my camera for a walk, and I've even tried pickleball. And to my surprise, it was fun! I took my mind off of my problems long enough to enjoy myself.

She smiled faintly to herself. *I've proven I can take steps,* she thought. *Now it's time to understand where they're leading.*

The thought carried both excitement and weight. Leina's words about awareness and intention echoed in her mind—it wasn't just about movement anymore. It was about meaning.

When they met again, Maureen told her, "I feel like I've been gathering pieces—insights, experiences, little sparks—I'm not sure how they fit together. But I feel like the fog has lifted!"

Leina nodded, her expression warm. "That's exactly where you should be. You've stepped through the fog, Maureen. You're standing on the bridge now. The next step is about shaping where it leads—turning awareness into direction."

Maureen tilted her head. "Direction sounds big."

"It doesn't have to be," Leina said gently. "Think of it as giving form to what's already unfolding. You've tried things, paid attention to what makes you feel alive. Now we'll begin to design around that—what you want to nurture, what you want to experience more of. It's less about control and more about conscious creation."

"That feels... possible," Maureen said quietly. "A little scary, but possible."

Leina smiled. "Fear isn't failure. It's often a sign that you're on the edge of something that matters. The real question isn't whether it's safe—it's whether it feels *aligned*. You'll know the difference."

Something inside Maureen settled. She realized that she was building forward, from this point on, and that she was well equipped for the journey.

Later that evening, as she sat by the window, her eyes drifted to her camera resting on the table. She thought of the bridge—the one she'd photographed so many times—and how it seemed to capture everything she was feeling: connection, transition, possibility. Maybe it was time to see those images differently. Maybe they held part of the story she was still learning to tell.

I've proven to myself I can take steps, she thought. *Now it's time to understand what I'm building.*

The realization gave her a quiet thrill. Leina's words echoed in her mind—*awareness first, then intention.* Maybe that's what this next stage was about: not just noticing, but choosing.

***

When they met again, Maureen could hardly wait to share.

"You're in a new phase now," Leina said with a knowing smile. "You are standing on the bridge. You've tried new things, you've paid attention to what feels alive—and now, it's time to start shaping where that bridge leads."

"Shaping it how?"

"By bringing intention to what you've already started. You've explored, reflected, experimented. Now it's about setting gentle priorities—defining what matters most and how you want your next steps to feel. We're not forcing action; we're giving direction to what's already unfolding."

Maureen nodded slowly. "That sounds… grounded. But still a little scary."

Leina smiled. "That's natural. Fear isn't a stop sign—it's an invitation to listen more closely. The question isn't 'am I afraid,' it's 'does this feel aligned?' You'll know the difference."

"So, this is where I start architecting the bridge? You know, to take me from where I am today to where I want to go?

"Exactly," Leina said. "You've done a lot of work—you've gained insights from your current life, you have explored what lights you up, you've deepened your appreciations for your experiences, you have greeted curiosity. Now we'll begin to design what connects where you are to where you want to be."

***

When she developed the film in her camera, the sense of wonder she experienced yesterday returned as she saw the bridge come to life in her photos. For some reason, it called to her, and it didn't escape her that she was at the entrance of her own bridge, one between her past and her future. Like Leina said, it was up to her to determine the path she wanted to take.

Her career was one thing that she needed to address. In retrospect, she could see that her previous career was a job, a safe job. She knew what she was doing, and she did it well, to the point that she functioned on autopilot most of the time. At the end, it hadn't been personally rewarding. It was a paycheck. It offered certainty and stability. But it really wasn't rewarding. So perhaps Leina was right—trusting her instincts and turning down a position that didn't excite her had been the right thing to do.

But she also knew that the perfect job wouldn't come knocking at her door. She had to find it. Maybe she had to create it.

She wondered if she could make photography a career. Possibly open a studio. But she dismissed that thought almost as soon as it came to her. Photography had always been a passion, but it was deeply personal to her. It fueled her creativity but it wasn't something she wanted to do professionally. At least not full time. Posed pictures were so boring! And owning a business involved more risk than she wanted to take. Plus, *I don't want to be a starving artist* she thought.

But there were other careers, and while it was scary to think about making a huge shift, she kept reminding herself that fear was not a reason to not consider something new. She needed something that was in alignment, like Leina had mentioned.

To Maureen, that was an entirely new way of thinking…

11

By the end of the next week, Maureen had a plan. While she still didn't know what she wanted to do with her career, she knew it was time to make a move—but to do that, she needed help.

So, she contacted the recruiter at the temp agency where she'd applied shortly after losing her job. She was ready to expand her career search beyond what she'd always known and done and thought the recruiter might be able to provide her with some guidance. At the very least, she hoped to discover other options that she hadn't previously entertained.

As a firm believer that appearances mattered, Maureen scoured her closet for the appointment. Not too formal … but not too casual. Finding something in between was difficult as she debated blue versus gray. Should she wear a jacket or not? It was times like these when she wished she had someone she could call and get their opinion.

Then she remembered that she did. Her daughter had always had good taste in clothing, and as she recalled, she had never been shy about telling her mom when she did or didn't like something she was wearing.

Laying a few outfits out on her bed, she facetimed her.

"Hi, Mom, what's up?"

"Hi, hon. I don't mean to bother you, but I have an appointment with a recruiter, and I can't seem to make up my mind about what to wear. I've pulled out a few things and wondered if you have a minute to give me your opinion," Maureen said, trying to sound nonchalant.

"Sure, let's take a look."

Scanning her phone's camera across her choices, she explained that she pulled those pieces because they could all mix and match.

"It's been a while, and I'm not as fashion savvy as I used to be," she laughed.

"Mom, they're all okay. But that's the problem — they're just okay. Nothing stands out. Nothing is memorable. I think you're playing it too safe. The light blue blouse goes with the gray slacks, but don't you have anything with a little more personality — a little more style?"

"Like what?" Maureen asked.

"Well, if you're going to wear neutral colors, do you have a belt or a pair of shoes that you can add to give the look a pop of color? It doesn't take much — you can wear any color and with the right accessories, you'll look more pulled together," her daughter suggested.

"Let's see, I have grey, brown, and black shoes. Oh, and there's that pair of red flats that I bought to wear to the company's Christmas party a couple years ago," Maureen replied.

"Yes! And that red clutch that you bought to go with it. Wear that!"

Maureen could hear the excitement in her daughter's voice.

Chuckling, she said, "Okay, but with which outfit?"

"Oh, your white button-down blouse and black slacks. No jacket. You'll look professional, but fashionable."

"I would've never picked red, but if you really think so…"

"I do. Everything else there is *boring*, Mom. Maybe it's time for you to update your wardrobe."

"Perhaps, but as you can see, I tend to play it safe. I'll probably end up with more of the same."

"Just try to mix it up. Have a little fun with it. Even if it's some bold jewelry, create your own style. And if you're not sure what looks good, give me a shout. I'll try to help," her daughter offered.

"I will do that," Maureen said. "Thanks for your advice."

"Sure thing, Mom. Now, get dressed and send me a selfie!"

Once dressed, a glance in her full-length mirror proved that her daughter was right. The red accessories weren't overpowering at all. They actually made her outfit look more polished and professional.

It was all so new to her. But so were meetings with recruiters and changing careers and being single.

"Have fun with it," her daughter had said. Was that what Leina had been telling her to do—to allow herself to have some fun, try new things, and feel some joy? To let go of the person she once was so she could grow into someone she wanted to be?

Funny how everyone can see it but me…

***

Explaining her goal to Beth, her recruiter, wasn't easy.

"I'm willing to explore other options, either a different career or a different industry, but I'm not sure what I'm qualified to do. I was hoping you could help me," Maureen shared.

For the next hour, they discussed her experience and browsed through job openings.

"Let's see, maybe something in accounting or bookkeeping," Beth suggested. "Either that or something business-related. Your experience as a data analyst would lend itself to something along those lines. Here's one—an executive assistant in hospital administration. Oh, wait, it says they prefer someone with healthcare experience or knowledgeable in medical terminology."

Both women looked up when they were approached by a man wearing a nametag that read "Craig."

"Excuse me, Beth, sorry to interrupt. Any luck filling the temp position for the juvenile program?"

"Not yet, but I'm looking. Most people are looking for full-time permanent employment, so it's going to be tough," Beth replied.

"Well, we are running out of time. The position will be vacant soon, and we need to get someone in there, or the program will have to shut down," Craig reminded her. "Take another look through the resumes this afternoon if you get a chance, please."

"I promise," Beth nodded.

Turning back to Maureen, she apologized.

"I'm sorry about that. Now, where were we?"

"Umm, you were going through some job opportunities, but I lacked the medical background. Can I ask about the position you were just talking about—the temp one?" Maureen replied.

"Well, it's a three-month position, basically supervising juveniles who got in trouble and opted to take part in a trial community service program, instead of taking their chances in front of a judge," Beth explained.

"Interesting, so why is it only three months?"

"The program is designed to run for six months, but the current director is moving out of state because her husband is being transferred. It's a tough position to fill since it's short-term, and it's also only a couple days a week."

"What does it entail?" Maureen continued to ask questions.

"Most of the work has been done. The teens have taken a class and are now required to get their community service hours in. The director has to monitor those hours and make sure they stay on track. There are some kids who want to get it done and behind them as soon as possible, but there are always those slackers who put it off until the last minute. The director has to verify their hours, keep them on target, review the weekly updates on their performance, and even find new opportunities for them to get their hours in if necessary. Maureen, are you interested?"

"Well, I did want a full-time position, but I'm not ruling anything out just yet," Maureen admitted.

"Hmm, you appear to be qualified with your experience working with numbers," Beth stated.

"Oh, there's more to it than calculating numbers. We had to analyze the information and apply it to specific goals, projecting outcomes, and…"

"Seeing if those goals would be met? That's a big part of this role, Maureen. But do you have experience working with teens?"

"I raised two," Maureen laughed. "So, I'd say yes."

"Let's look at the job posting. It's two to three days a week, they prefer someone with supervisory experience, who enjoys working with youth, and … oh, wait, they prefer someone with volunteer experience," Beth said with disappointment. "Your resume doesn't indicate you have any."

"Oh, but I do! I was on the board of the PTA when my kids were in school, and I'm now volunteering at the shelter on the west side of town, making food and serving lunch for the homeless and needy," Maureen shared.

"Really? Would you consider this job? We'd need someone who can start rather quickly, and we're really looking for someone who will see the program through to its end, so we don't have to look for someone else to replace them, too. And don't forget, it is temporary *and* part-time," Beth reminded her.

"I think I am interested. And I could commit to it for three months," Maureen said, her voice becoming more confident.

"Well, then, we have some work to do," Beth said, placing Maureen's resume in front of her. "We need to update your resume to include your volunteer work and get you an interview."

"Who will be interviewing me?"

"Delilah Brown, the current director of the program, and Judge Erickson, who is overseeing the youth. And, of course, Craig, who you just briefly met. Let me go get him; he's going to be so excited!"

***

Three days later, when Maureen officially accepted the position, she texted her daughter.

"Hi. Just wanted to thank you for the fashion advice. It seems that red might be my lucky color — I just accepted a part-time position as the director of a youth program. Thank you!"

"Wow, Mom. That's great! But it doesn't sound like anything you've done before. Maybe you can tell me more about it when I come home for Libby's wedding shower next month."

"Libby is getting married? You're coming home?"

"Yes and yes. I must've forgotten to mention it. Is it okay if I stay with you that weekend?"

"Of course you can."

"Great! Maybe we can get a little clothes shopping in while I'm there."

Later that night, Maureen smiled as she imagined what Leina would say. *Do you see what can happen when you don't wait for whatever the future has in store, and instead, become a participant in creating your own future? Maureen, you're writing your own Treasure Map to Joy™. I'm excited to see where it takes you!*

12

Excited and anxious at the same time, Maureen was determined to make a good impression in her new position. On day one, she found that she had a lot to learn, and she also discovered that the role had challenges that she needed to navigate on her own.

Maureen was expected to meet twice weekly with the youth members as a group and individually. The meetings were scheduled for Wednesday afternoons and Saturday mornings, and she was told they would be held in a meeting room in the basement of City Hall. However, when she contacted them about the schedule, they told her that the planning committee had reserved the room on Wednesdays for the next month, and she would have to find an alternative place to meet.

 But where?

Asking around, she was told that she could go into the system and insert a room request, but it was up to her find a room to request.

To her dismay, there weren't any available. Not knowing where to turn, she asked what her options were.

She was told that there weren't any rules ... as long as the requirements were fulfilled.

Mulling over the situation, it occurred to her that City Hall wasn't an option. She had to find another place, and quickly.

Then, she remembered that the shelter had a community room that was underutilized. Picking up the phone, she called Jo.

"Well, I don't see why not, Maureen. But it's not up to me. You'll have to clear it with Mark, of course," Jo said. "Here's his number. Give him a call."

Thirty minutes later, she had rescheduled all of their Wednesday meetings to the community room and had sent a notification to the group informing them of the new meeting place.

That done, she settled in to review the files. Sixteen youth members had entered the program when it began, and here in the last two months, they were down to 12. The majority of them were meeting the requirements to successfully complete the program and, therefore, would not receive any additional fine or sentence for their wrongdoings, but there were three who were definitely falling behind, and it was her job to get them on track again.

The job also held "other expectations," one of which was to attend monthly Chamber of Commerce meetings to garner additional support for the program from leaders of the community and, perhaps, seek organizations who would be willing to sponsor their youth members.

In her first Chamber of Commerce meeting, Maureen introduced herself and assured the members that she would help them in any way. If they were having difficulties or conflicts that prevented them from fulfilling their commitments, she needed to know.

Then, she met with each chamber member separately and the individuals supervising their community service. It was quite informative, and Maureen's head was spinning with the number of people she'd met in a few short hours.

"Welcome to the team, Maureen," said Anna, the Human Resource Director of the local hospital. "If there's anything I can do or if you have any questions, give me a call."

"Thank you. And I just might take you up on that. I feel like I have a lot of catching up to do."

"You'll be fine," Anna smiled. "The chamber meetings can be boring sometimes. But we try to make the best of it. There's a group of us that always hit Antonio's for pizza after the meeting. You're welcome to join us if you'd like."

"I just might do that. It will give me a chance to know a few people better," Maureen said.

***

Throughout the next couple weeks, she had the opportunity to spend more time at the Community Center and, therefore, got to know Mark better.

One day, she found him in his office late in the day and asked him what was keeping him there so late. Exasperated, he sighed and mumbled something about filing and catching up on paperwork—something he wanted to make sure was done before his replacement was found.

"It would be nice to have some office help," he said. "I'm afraid I'm not too organized and it piled up on me."

Offering to help, Maureen noticed that many of the reports had been handwritten on forms.

"You're not submitting your reports electronically?" she asked.

"No, I'm not that tech savvy, I guess. It's easier for me to fill in the numbers and mail them. Perhaps my replacement will tackle that one, but it's too late for me."

***

Maureen quickly discovered that one of the girls in the youth program hung around longer than the rest.

"You're free to go, Tonya," she said after their first meeting.

"If it's okay, I'm going to stick around a while," she said. "My mom can't pick me up until she gets off work."

"Oh, well, sure. I'll just be down the hall if you need anything."

Thirty minutes later, Maureen walked into the community room to find Tonya at a table, pencil in hand.

"Homework?" she asked.

"Oh, no. I'm just drawing," the girl said quietly.

"Mind if I take a look?" Maureen peered over her shoulder.

"Tonya, this is very good. Incredible even. You're quite the artist," she remarked.

"It's just a pencil drawing. I don't have my watercolors here," Tonya humbly replied.

"Well, I'm impressed. It really is quite good," Maureen said before walking away, not wanting to make the girl uncomfortable.

Sitting at a nearby table, Maureen took the opportunity to review some paperwork. A few minutes later, Tonya softly spoke.

"I was hungry," she said.

"Pardon me?"

"I was hungry. That's why I got in trouble. I stole some food so my brother and I could eat."

"Oh my," Maureen said, not certain how to respond.

"Do your parents know that's what you were doing?" she asked.

"I didn't say anything, but I think my mom knows. She works hard and really tries. But sometimes there isn't enough money," Tonya said, once again so softly that Maureen had to strain to hear.

"And your father?" Maureen asked.

"He ditched us. Said he couldn't deal and took off a few years ago. He doesn't help us, and we never see him. I just wanted to eat, that's all. I'm not a bad person," Tonya said.

"Of course, you aren't. And I'm sorry that you were in that position. Did you know that there are places where you can get a free meal, no questions asked? One of them is right here in this building. And you can bring your brother … and your mom," Maureen informed her, now sitting by her side.

She handed Tonya a flyer with the days and hours, and even managed to run to the kitchen, where she grabbed a few of those sandwiches that are usually ready for the occasional person who walks in after hours.

"Here, take these, and I found a few pieces of fruit, too. If you've already eaten, you can save them for lunch tomorrow."

The encounter touched Maureen, and it occurred to her that maybe she was in the right place at the right time. She only knew that she was grateful that she could help.

It was something she brought up to her daughter when she came home for her friend's bridal shower.

"I feel like she shouldn't even be in the program," she admitted.

"Mom, I agree. Most kids do something that they aren't proud of. It doesn't make them a bad person. It's like the time I got arrested, and I'm not a troublemaker," Sophie said.

"Wait—arrested?" Maureen asked, unsure if she had heard her daughter correctly. "What do you mean, arrested?"

"It was nothing, really. It was a few years ago, and nothing to worry about."

"No, stop. What happened? Why didn't I know?"

"Mom, it was my freshman year at college, and there was a party. Everybody was drinking, and I decided to do it, too. We were just having fun, but then the cops came and asked for IDs, and I was arrested for underage drinking," Sophie said.

"Why didn't I know this?"

"Well, they released us with a warning, but only after we called our parents and told on ourselves. I called Dad," she meekly answered.

"Dad?" Maureen asked, surprised.

"Well, Mom, you were going through the divorce and selling the house. You were upset and sad, and I didn't want to disappoint you or make matters worse for you, so I called Dad, and he took care of everything. It's over and done."

It was a lot for Maureen to take in. Hearing that her daughter didn't feel comfortable confiding in her was tough. Knowing that her emotional state had caused her kids to be cautious with her hurt. But rather than questioning her daughter any further, she apologized.

"I'm sorry. I didn't realize that I was so wrapped up in my situation that it wasn't comfortable for you. I never intended for you to feel like you weren't important to me. Honey, I hope you know that you can come to me, no matter what is happening in my life. Or no matter what you've done," she reassured Sophie.

"Thanks, but don't worry. It never happened again. Besides, I'm 21 now, so it's all good. Now, I've got to get ready for the shower. Maybe we can grab something to eat later?"

"Sure, figure out where you want to go and let me know," Maureen said, still processing what her daughter had told her.

"How about The Pier? I've been craving their crab cakes—they're sooo good!"

Suddenly, Maureen froze. The Pier had always been their go-to restaurant, and the four of them had enjoyed many dinners there throughout the years. She hadn't been back since the divorce.

Sensing her mother's hesitation, Sophie jumped back in.

"If you'd rather not, that's okay. I'm sorry—I didn't mean…"

"No, no. It's okay. The Pier it is! I haven't had their salmon in quite a while. I can make reservations for two for what, 8:00 sound okay?" Maureen suggested.

"Sure," Sophie smiled. "And Mom?"

"Yes?"

"Thanks. Sometimes I forget…"

"Don't say another word. I'm fine, really, I am," Maureen quickly dismissed her daughter's concerns.

"If you're sure," Sophie said. "But I won't forget that we're going shopping tomorrow. I'm not leaving town until we bring your wardrobe into this decade!"

"It's a date," Maureen laughed. "Now, go have a good time at the shower, while I go see if there's anything I can wear that doesn't look like it came from the 80's."

13

"How was your visit with Sophie?" Jo asked as they stood at the counter peeling the last of the potatoes.

"It was good. We went to The Pier for dinner. Neither one of us had been there since the di …. We hadn't been there for a couple years. It was nice to go back and enjoy some of our favorite dishes. And then we went shopping the next morning—well, Sophie shopped. I just tried on whatever she threw at me and had the pleasure of paying for it."

"Your daughter picked out clothes for you? Usually it's the other way around," Jo pointed out.

"That's for sure. Apparently, that role switches when they grow up. Instead of me approving what she wears in public, she now has to approve what I wear in public," she laughed.

"I bet you had a lot to catch up on," said Jo.

"I guess. We talked about my new job a bit."

"How's that going? Do you like it?" Jo asked.

"I do. I'm learning a lot, especially that our community doesn't have the resources that some of these kids need. Jo, I swear half of the kids in the program wouldn't be there if we did."

"Like what?"

"Umm, like mentors, supervised age-appropriate activities, role models, even accessible tutors. They need direction, not punishment, and I truly believe that. One girl, though, she doesn't even need that—she needed something to eat. She stole food because she and her brother were hungry. It made me realize just how important what you do here really is. She seemed a bit ashamed when she told me, and I was so grateful that I knew all about this program and gave her all the information … and a few sandwiches from the kitchen. Hopefully, she'll never feel like she has to resort to stealing again."

"It happens more than you think, Maureen," Jo nodded.

"It doesn't need to. There has to be a way to let the public know that we're here, and they don't have to go hungry or eat out of trash cans," Maureen said.

"We all could do better, Maureen, but we can't do it all," said Jo.

"I know, but it just doesn't seem like enough."

***

Jo's words continued to tug at Maureen. *If we can't do it all, then who can?* she wondered.

She made a list of the things she'd mentioned to Jo: obtaining mentors, finding motivational speakers, creating activities, maybe even offering training or classes, and, of course, making sure the public was aware that there were kitchens and resources for those who needed it. Then, she took the liberty of adding a few more items to her "wish list," such as improving the community building, sprucing it up with paint and making it available to the public for events, activities, and even shelter.

What would it take? Money … and time, lots of time.

The next time she saw Mark, she approached him with her ideas.

"Those are all good ideas, Maureen," he said, "but the funding isn't there. I can't afford to tackle one of those things, let alone all of them. Besides, I'm at the end of my tenure here. If anything at all were to happen, it would be up to my replacement. Maybe you should wait and take it up with the next guy."

Knowing that Mark wasn't on board, Maureen wasn't ready to throw in the towel—not just yet. So, when she went to the Chamber of Commerce meeting that month, she brought it up to the group as they waited for their pizza at Antonio's.

"Those are great ideas!"

"Hey, why don't you ask for donations from companies in the area? My employer agreed to sponsor a member for community service. They might be willing to invest some money in the community."

The positive feedback continued. In the end, Maureen agreed to keep in touch, letting them know if and when they might be needed.

***

When she met with Leina, Maureen updated her coach, telling her everything that had happened in the last two weeks. She started with her visit with Sophie and went on to tell her about the youth program, making sure to share her exchange with Tonya and how it invoked her desire to do more to serve the community.

"That's a lot to unpack, Maureen. Let's start with Sophie. It sounds like a good visit. I think you are making headway," Leina said.

"Perhaps. It was so good to see her and spend some time together, but to be honest, it feels like we are both playing it safe, trying not to say or do anything to rock the boat," Maureen admitted.

Leina nodded thoughtfully, then spoke. "I'm sure you want a deeper connection with your children, and that's natural. But rebuilding relationships—especially the ones that matter most—means allowing them to become someone new. You just have to keep showing up, without the need to control how it unfolds. Let it breathe. Let it become what it wants to be. The two of you will redefine your relationship as you both move forward in this. It might not look like it did before, but that doesn't mean it can't be meaningful—or even better."

"I just feel like Sophie is waiting for me to wave a magic wand and, ta-da, everything will go back to normal," Maureen sighed.

"Is Sophie wanting that—or is it you, Maureen?" Leina asked gently.

Maureen blinked, caught off guard by the question.

"That's a lot of pressure to put on yourself," Leina continued. "There isn't a magic wand—and there doesn't need to be. Your kids don't need you to have all the answers; they just need you to be real with them. Sometimes the most healing thing you can offer is your honesty, not your solutions."

Maureen nodded slowly. "Then what do I need to do? I'm just not sure anymore."

Leina smiled softly. "Start where you are. You've already taken the first steps. Keep showing up as yourself—as the woman who's learning, growing, and trying. It will look different, yes, but that doesn't mean it will be less fulfilling. It might be more than you ever imagined."

Leina then turned the conversation to Maureen's job.

"How do you feel about your new job?" she asked.

"Good. At first, I thought I might be in over my head, but I gained my footing and I'm really beginning to like what I'm doing. I believe in the program and really want to help these kids get on the right path. And I have to admit that I'm surprised that I'm actually enjoying getting to know the sponsors and business representatives that participate. I was even happy that I went to the Chamber of Commerce meeting—I can't tell you how long it's been since I had pizza with fiends!"

"Friends?" Leina asked, smiling.

After a brief pause, Maureen smiled.

"Yes, friends. Not close friends, but we had a good time, and I look forward to seeing them again," Maureen said.

"Look how far you've come. Wasn't it just six months ago that you didn't have a job, your days were long and empty, and you hadn't talked to your children for too long? And look at you now—Maureen, you are truly creating your Treasure Map to Joy™ and you're finding your way beautifully!" Leina exclaimed.

"I am getting there, Leina. It would all be good if I wasn't so frustrated with the lack of resources for those who are underserved. And then I remind myself that I only have this job for another month before the grant ends, and I'll be back where I started, except I will still volunteer and work with Jo and the gang. It seems like I take one step forward and then two steps back."

"But each step you take forward takes you closer to where you want to be. That progress cannot be undone, as long as you intentionally seek those things that will bring you joy. Remember, your dream job won't come knocking on your door. The resources and tools you need won't just fall out of the sky. You have to be an active participant in getting what you want. So, my next question, Maureen, is how are you going to make those things happen?"

Maureen paused, gently biting her lip in deep thought. Then the answer came to her as if it had always been there, just waiting for her to ask it to step forward.

"It's all coming together," she said. "The only way I can make all those things happen is to manage the Community Service Center. I want Mark's job!"

Maureen's excitement didn't wane during the ride home. It made so much sense. Everything had led her directly to this place, this job, this opportunity. All she had to do seize it.

Before she changed her mind, she sent Mark a text.

"Hi, Mark. I wanted you to know that I am interested in becoming the new CSC Director when you retire. What do I need to do?"

A few minutes later, he replied.

"Stop by my office tomorrow, and I'll give you the details."

14

Maureen was excited when her feet hit the floor the next morning. She felt confident and excited about going in and letting Mark know that she really wanted take over the reins when he retired. It was just logical, almost perfect. Her path had led her right to the position, and as a result, Mark had gotten to know her well enough that he would agree that she was the perfect one for the job.

Smiling as she clasped on a bracelet that perfectly accentuated her new outfit, she realized that Sophia was right. The woman in the mirror did look professional, but still stylish. Her new clothes would serve her well in her new position, she thought, as she gave herself one last glimpse in the mirror.

***

Mark was pouring a cup of coffee when she walked through his door.

"Good morning, Maureen," he said. "Coffee?"

"Yes, thank you."

"So, you're interested in running this not-for-profit? You're sure this is what you want?" he asked.

"Yes, Mark. I've thought it over, and I really feel this is the right next step for me," she said.

"Well, then," he said, pulling open a file cabinet drawer. "You'll need this … and let's see, this … oh, and consent for a background test."

"What's this?" she asked, staring at the papers before her.

"Well, there's the application you need to fill out, and…"

"Application? Have others applied?" she asked, confused.

"Last I heard, I'd say half a dozen or so, maybe more," Mark shrugged. The board wants to weed them out by the end of the week and start interviews next week, so you should probably get the paperwork submitted in the next day or two."

"Um, okay. Yes, I'll make sure to do that," Maureen said, trying to hide the fact that she was flustered.

She kicked herself the entire way home.

How could I be so naïve? Of course, they're going to interview people! What was I thinking – that I'd walk in and, ta-da, they would give me the job?

And I let myself get my hopes up when it's obvious that I probably cannot compete with the other applicants. I don't have the experience or the education for this position. I don't deserve it, and I certainly haven't done anything to earn it. I should bow out now and save myself the embarrassment of not getting the job.

Maureen had mistakenly fallen into a false sense of security. She had made a name and place for herself at the shelters and felt like one of the family. After spending weeks working with youth at the Community Center, she had come to feel at home there, as well. Somehow, in her comfortable environment, she felt so accepted that to her it was a given that she would step in and fill Mark's shoes.

Boy, was she wrong.

And she told Leina so.

"I'm just so embarrassed. What was I thinking? Of course this will be a competitive position, and I have to admit that I'm not qualified. I don't deserve it, Leina."

"Really? You have to look at other things besides your resume. There are your life experiences, your ability to overcome adversity, your willingness to serve … and then there's the service aspect. I don't know anyone more qualified to serve than you — I've seen how rewarding you find it and how it motivates you every day. Maybe you are more qualified than you think, Maureen," Leina suggested.

"What if applying makes me a laughingstock? What if this is not the right decision, and it actually sets me back, undoing everything I've done so far?"

"There is no 'right' decision — only the next step that feels most aligned. I think you have to agree that this does feel aligned with the path you've been on. Am I right?"

"I suppose so," Maureen reluctantly agreed.

"In that case, I hope you reconsider. I think you are qualified, and I think the board might agree. You have a vision and passion that are likely unmatched, not to mention tons of ideas. The answers you are looking for are inside you. I'm just here to help you hear them. And while it is true that we are referring to your quest for joy, the journey is applicable to everything else---if those things can bring you joy, as well. "

"Leina, I feel like a kid again … I'm scared to put myself out there, scared of being rejected," admitted Maureen.

"I get it. You feel vulnerable — we all do from time to time," Leina said gently. "When that happens, I remind myself of one thing: don't make decisions from fear. Make them from alignment. And if something feels aligned, trust it."

"Okay. Let me consider that" Maureen said.

"Sleep on it, Maureen. I think the answer will reveal itself to you. And when it does, trust it."

***

After a long night, Maureen finally came to a conclusion — she would not let fear rob her of the joy she is entitled to. She knew it was out there, somewhere, and maybe she was on the right track. But she would never know if she gave up because she was afraid that she was on the wrong path … or worse, unworthy.

Before she could change her mind, she filled out the application and uploaded the documents. Attaching them to the email, she applied for the position that she knew she dearly wanted but feared she wouldn't get.

Hitting send, she told herself that time would tell if she was doing the right thing. And again, she reminded herself that time was one thing she'd had plenty of.

Maybe, just maybe, this time it would be on her side.

15

Two days later, Maureen received a phone call to set up an interview with the board. Deciding to get it over with rather than dragging out her anxiety, she took the first interview slot offered: the next Wednesday at 9:00 a.m. sharp.

In the meantime, she intentionally kept herself busy. With just a few weeks left working with the teens, she threw herself into making sure they met their requirements to successfully complete the program. Tonya was doing well. Her school counselor reported that her grades were good, and Maureen was happy to see that she had completed her community service hours in the first month. To Maureen, the kid was in no danger of repeating her crime, and the conversations they had reinforced that belief.

Yes, Tonya was still remaining at the Community Center after their meetings were over. And Maureen was happy to oblige — she was safe there, and her mother always picked her up as soon as her shift at the convenience store ended. Besides, it gave

Maureen an opportunity to see the young girl's painting come to life.

"Look," Tonya had said the week before. "My art teacher said I could take these paints home so I could complete my picture, as long as I promise to bring them back when I'm done."

"That's wonderful, Tonya! I'm really excited to see it when it's done. It's already beautiful. You have quite a gift," Maureen replied, honestly impressed.

There were a couple of teens, though, who were in danger of not meeting their requirements, which meant their case would ultimately go before a judge for an alternate "sentence." Maureen's goal was to help the teens, but it was also to provide the direction and support to make the program itself a success. Because it was a one-time grant, this first group of kids were considered a trial run, and the continuance of the program would depend on whether it was deemed an overall success.

Because she owed it to the kids, she needed to find places where they could complete their hours. After reaching out to her network from the Chamber of Commerce, she realized that the quick turnaround in time would be a problem.

Perhaps they could volunteer at one of the kitchens … or maybe there was something they could do at the Community Center. Then, it hit her.

The room where they met, the one that was underutilized, needed a makeover. It was in dire need of an updated look and a deep cleaning. The teens could clean and paint it on a weekend so it wouldn't interfere with their attendance at school. But there was just one problem—when she asked Mark, he said they had some money, but not enough to cover paint and supplies.

So, she got innovative. If the businesses and other organizations couldn't get clearances to bring the teens into their facilities, perhaps they'd be willing to donate toward the cause.

After sending a group email, the responses were quick.

A local hotel had just renovated their dining room and said they would donate the tables and chairs that had been replaced. The manager of the home improvement store was willing to donate the paint, and the maintenance department of the hospital agreed to provide them with paint brushes, rollers, and drop cloths. Several other businesses and organizations offered donations, as well. As Maureen saw it all coming together, she became excited. If it all panned out, not only would the teens meet their requirements and the grant be renewed, but the Community Center would gain a new, inviting room that the community would be proud to use.

***

The next Tuesday morning, Maureen nearly canceled her interview again when she learned from Mark that the competition was fierce. There was a young man who had graduated the year before with a Bachelor's in Business Management, and another applicant had been operating a not-for-profit organization for several years and, undoubtedly, had more experience than Maureen. And those were only two applicants that she knew about—she was certain there were others, more qualified and more experienced than she.

Then she remembered what Leina had told her early on—*Don't make decisions out of fear. Make them from alignment.*

As she sat with that thought, something in her heart steadied. Deep down, she knew this opportunity felt aligned with who she was becoming and the kind of life she wanted to create. It wasn't about certainty; it was about trust.

So, instead of stepping back out of fear, she chose to lean in with faith in herself. She'd already taken a few steps onto this new bridge—and she'd never know what waited on the other side if she turned back now.

Copies of her resume in hand, she walked into the interview looking more confident than she felt. The board members were friendly and welcoming and started the interview with safe questions.

"Tell us about yourself."

"What is your experience?"

As she answered the questions, she knew she fell short of someone with years of experience and someone who was highly qualified with a framed degree ready to hang on the wall. Just when she was about to admit her shortcomings, they asked another question:

"What is your vision of the Community Service Center and its role within the community?"

Suddenly, Maureen came to life.

She told them that she thought it was underutilized and needed to be promoted more. After all, most people didn't know about the Center or the kitchens—she had stumbled across the kitchen by chance herself.

And she discussed the programs they could offer—events, fundraisers, activities for youth and seniors, resources for the underprivileged, and training programs, job fairs, and…

She didn't know if she listed them all because suddenly the board was asking for specifics and how she would fund an increase in services and resources. Their talk lasted another hour before they were interrupted — the next applicant had arrived.

Thanking her, they advised that they would make a decision within the next week.

And while Maureen walked away uncertain about her chances, she knew she had lit a spark of excitement when she spoke of growth and the future potential and impact that the Center could have on the residents.

Then she went back to work. They were painting the Community Service Center room that weekend, and she needed to pick up the supplies and be prepared.

To her delight, every teen in the program volunteered to help. They all arrived on time, ready to tackle the task at hand. And they did it without complaining. It even appeared they were having fun. The music was playing, and they were joking and laughing most of the day. When they completed the second coat, they stepped back and took pride in their work.

"You should be proud. And I'm proud of all of you. Every one of you completed the requirements to graduate from the program, and that is a major accomplishment! It's been wonderful working with you all," Maureen said.

Tonya then approached her.

"Maureen, I finished my painting, and I wanted to give it to you," she softly said.

Touched, Mauren almost accepted, but then remembered that it would be a conflict of interests.

"I am sorry. It is beautiful, and I would love to have it, but it wouldn't be ethical for me to accept a gift," she informed her.

"Oh." Tonya's disappointment was obvious.

"But I have an idea. Let me clear it first—I'll give you a phone call when I know what I *can* do."

***

The next Tuesday morning, Maureen received a phone call offering her the position of Community Service Center Director. They told her they were very impressed with her vision, saying they loved that she knew what she wanted the Center to look like five years down the road. And when they saw the newly renovated room at the Center, their decision was made.

This time, Maureen didn't have to check on anything. This was an offer she could accept … and she gladly did.

16

Eighteen Months Later....

Maureen had been anxious when she applied for the grant that would help them offer job fairs and training, but she was even more excited when the grant was approved. She had worked with city officials to offer services for youth and teens, and to her delight, the participation was very well received. The meeting room, now freshly painted with matching tables and chairs, was being utilized, and more calls were coming in every week inquiring about renting the space for various events and private parties.

It had even been given the nickname, "The Landmark Room," dubbed so because of the photographs of historic buildings, churches, and city structures that graced the walls. In the center, proudly displayed, was the photograph Maureen had taken of the wooden bridge that had captured her attention the first time she had visited the Center. To Maureen, it was symbolic of her own journey, one that led her from a past that she had been afraid to leave behind to a future of unknowns in which she was finding joy.

Initially, she had considered hanging photo behind her sofa, but seeing Tonya's painting sparked another idea. Leina had often repeated the need for her to ask herself, "How does that make me feel?" when making a decision. And while she was drawn to the bridge and everything it stood for, it didn't make her feel like Tonya's painting did — calm, serene, and warm. It truly was a work of art that brought her joy, which was why she waited until Tonya had graduated from the at-risk program to purchase it from her ... but not until she had done some research to determine a price that was fair. Tonya was elated that Maureen liked the landscape enough to pay for it, and Maureen's heart warmed at the pride on the young girl's face.

It was that painting that hung over her sofa, and she loved it as much today as she had the day she bought it.

***

It was a warm Saturday morning in late September, and she had just finished her weekly pickleball game.

"Nice dink, Maureen!" one of her opponents said. "How about a rematch?"

"I'd love to," she shot back, "but I have an appointment. Can I take a rain check?"

"Sure, you're on, next week, same time, same place."

"You got it!" she smiled as she gathered her things to leave.

Truth be told, any other day, she would have taken him up on the rematch. As she'd gotten to know the game, she found she really liked it. And to her surprise she was getting pretty good at it. Even more shocking, she was beginning to see a competitive side to herself — one that she'd never known existed before. It was all in good fun, but she found that she actually enjoyed winning.

Glancing at her watch, she picked up the pace. If she was going to get home in time to shower before her hair appointment, she would have to hustle.

As she approached her porch, she smiled, pleased with the work she'd done the weekend before. Now that the front door had a fresh coat of paint and a fresh fall wreath, it was all coming together. The mums she'd purchased as an afterthought were the perfect touch, making it feel warm and inviting — a far cry from what it had looked like the first time she saw it.

The day she hung her photograph of the bridge in the Center, she decided it was time to walk across that bridge to see what was on the other side. She knew it was an older part of town that had once housed a couple factories where a large section of the community worked and lived at the time. In the 70s, those factories closed their doors, and as residents relocated to find employment elsewhere, the homes were left empty and the surrounding neighborhoods took a hit. When the new highway was built, it routed traffic through the outskirts of town, and the housing became even less desirable for young families who sought newer suburban homes in the subdivisions that offered tracts of houses with modern amenities.

Camera in hand, Maureen set out for an exploration.

She hadn't intended to look for anything in particular — just another afternoon with her camera, following her curiosity wherever it led. Lost in time, she wandered through an old part of town where a row of small houses stood shoulder to shoulder, some weathered and forgotten, others showing signs of renewal.

As she lifted her camera, she wondered what life might have been like here years ago—the laughter, the stories, the dreams once held behind these doors. Through the lens, she framed a doorway, adjusting her focus—and that's when she saw it.

A *For Sale* sign.

Lowering the camera, Maureen blinked, taking in the house as if seeing it for the first time. Something about it tugged at her—familiar yet full of possibility.

It was love at first sight. The two-bedroom cottage spoke to her immediately, and she marveled at the gables and the small covered porch. It was like taking a step back in time, and Maureen closed her eyes and envisioned the house with a fresh coat of paint and flowers growing alongside the brick walkway leading to the front door.

That very night, she called the number and scheduled a tour.

As the realtor led her though the empty house, she noted the details—wide plank hardwood floors, solid oak doors and trim throughout. It was small, but charming—even the kitchen that definitely needed updating and the bathroom, which still had its original pink tiles on the walls, didn't discourage her from wanting to put in an offer.

Her son tried to discourage her reminding her that an old home could be a money pit. When she didn't cave, he gave in, making her promise that she'd get a home inspection before she did anything.

As she occasionally still did, she reached out to Leina, wondering if she was moving too fast or making a decision for the wrong reason. After all, it was a major investment, the biggest one she'd ever make on her own. What if it was a mistake? What if she would regret it down the road?

And Leina reminded her that taking conscious action toward what we want can be scary. But she applauded her for doing it. Then, she asked the pivotal question, "How does the house make you *feel*, Maureen?"

"It makes me feel like I'm at home, like I belong, and I haven't felt that way for a long time," she admitted. "Yes, there is work to do, but I can see the possibilities!"

Three months later, she moved into her new home, and she didn't regret it a bit. She admired the living room when she walked in the door, and she smiled when she saw Tonya's painting hanging over her sofa. It brought her joy every day.

***

Late that afternoon, she emerged from her bedroom in the new evening gown she bought especially for the occasion. The city was turning 150 years old, and the occasion was being celebrated at a gala that would be attended by city officials, business owners, and some of the most prestigious people around town. Initially, Maureen hesitated before confirming her attendance, fearing it would be awkward to attend such an event alone. But then she reminded herself how far she had come, and before she could change her mind, she sent in her RSVP.

To her delight, she was seated at a table with a group of people she knew from the months attending Chamber of Commerce meetings, and she quickly felt at ease.

The speeches began, and the key players in city government were recognized for their contributions throughout the years. Then everyone who made the event possible was recognized and thanked, before the mayor announced one last award.

"We now welcome two special guests to announce our last award recipient," he said.

Maureen's breath was taken away when she saw two people emerging from the sidelines, hand in hand.

It was Jake and Sophie. Her kids.

Her eyes welled with tears as she listened to her children introduce their mother, explaining that she had always been a giving and compassionate person who strived to do what was best for their family and community. They spoke of her selfless nature and how she had always put others first. Then they listed her achievements as Director of the Community Service Center, before presenting the award.

"It is with great pride that we introduce you to the recipient of this year's award," Sophie smiled broadly as she turned to her brother, who spoke next.

"The Good Samaritan of the Year award goes to our mother, Maureen James," Jake announced.

As the crowd applauded, a stunned Maureen was called up to the stage. On shaky legs, she crossed the stage and walked into the waiting arms of her children.

"You look stunning!" Sophie whispered in her ear.

"Congratulations, Mom. We are proud of you," Jake said, hugging her tightly.

It was at that moment that Maureen knew she had never been prouder of them. They had grown to become strong, beautiful, independent adults, just like they were supposed to be.

And for the first time, she was aware that she had everything she ever wanted. It wasn't the award, the house, or the career — it was a culmination of those things—a feeling that she was right where she wanted to be at that moment in time. It had been a journey of growth and exploration, but, with Leina's guidance, Maureen had charted her own map —and in doing so, had discovered life's greatest treasure.

And what a joyous treasure it was!

a note from the author

Every story is really two stories: the one on the written page and the one it awakens in us.

For that reason, I invite you to pause for a moment and reflect on your experience as you traveled with Maureen on her journey from disruption to joy. Did you recognize parts of yourself in her story? Did it echo moments of your own life? What emotions quietly surfaced as you walked alongside her?

These questions matter because the way we experience a story often mirrors the way we experience life. As you reflect on what this book stirred within you, I'd like to share what joy has come to mean for me—not as a fleeting spark, but as a deeper, steadier presence that I return to again and again. One that is available to you, too.

The Nature of Joy

Joy, for me, is not the same as happiness. Although we often conflate the two, they are distinctly different. Happiness usually depends on external circumstances: a good day, an achievement, a shared laugh. Joy is something else entirely. It is a state of being that endures beyond circumstances, one that can exist alongside sadness, grief, or even uncertainty. If happiness is like a wave on the surface of the ocean, joy is the current that moves beneath, steady and constant.

Another truth I've discovered is that joy is both universal and deeply personal. The longing for it lives within every one of us, but the way it shows up is as unique as our own fingerprints.

What awakens joy for me may not do the same for you, and that's as it should be. And because of that, joy cannot be prescribed or defined by others. It isn't about living up to someone else's idea of what life should look like, or chasing what the world tells us will make us happy. It isn't dictated by society, culture, circumstances, institutions, or other people's approval. True joy rises from within when we honor what makes us feel most alive, most connected, and most true to ourselves.

Joy as Your Compass

Here's the beautiful truth: joy is always there. It doesn't have to be earned or chased. It lives within us, steady and available, waiting to be discovered—not only in the big milestones of life, but also in the small, everyday moments.

This is why I chose the imagery of a *Treasure Map to Joy*™. Just as a compass points us toward true north, joy can point us back to what is steady, life-giving, and true. For joy to guide us, we must first bring awareness to it. How? By choosing to look for it, to notice the moments that make us feel awake, alive, and connected. When we shift our attention toward joy, it naturally begins to guide us, reorienting us when we feel lost, reminding us of what truly matters. Even in the hardest of times—seasons of loss, transition, or change—joy can steady us, sustain us, and gently return us to ourselves.

Joy as Your Default

Over time, I've discovered something that changed the way I live: joy doesn't just come and go — it can become our default. For most of us, joy feels occasional and fleeting. But just as we can strengthen a muscle, we can strengthen our capacity for joy until it becomes the emotional ground we return to most naturally.

This doesn't mean we won't feel grief, anger, or fear. We are human, and those emotions are part of the landscape. What it does mean is that joy doesn't vanish when other feelings appear. It remains underneath them, steady and enduring. We can train ourselves to return to joy — not by denying our other emotions, but by allowing joy to coexist with them as a kind of home base.

Your Personal Map

Unlike a single fixed destination, your *Treasure Map to Joy*™ is deeply personal. Maureen's path was hers; yours will be yours. The treasures are not 'out there' waiting to be discovered. I truly believe they are already within you, waiting to be uncovered and claimed. And that's the heart of the work I do with my clients — helping them discover what has been within them all along.

My hope is that Maureen's story has offered you a glimpse of your own *Treasure Map to Joy*™ — helping you notice more clearly what brings you joy, as well as what dims it. In that way, the story encourages you to pay closer attention to your own life, to the patterns and possibilities already within you.

Joy is ready to walk beside you as a companion, guide you as a compass, and, when you allow it, steady you as your default state of being.

As you step back into your own story, may you carry this truth with you: joy is not out there somewhere, waiting to be found. It is here, within you, ready to be remembered, nurtured, and lived.

May joy always guide and nurture you,

Stacie

continue your journey

If this story stirred something in you — if you saw your own questions, patterns, or quiet longings reflected back — then maybe it's time to chart your next step with intention.

How?

The Clarity Sequence: Your Next Step on the Path to Joy

Transformation doesn't begin with a plan — it begins with awareness. A clear, compassionate look at where your life truly is and an authentic vision of where you want it to go.

The Clarity Sequence helps you do exactly that.

It's not a course.

It's not a quiz.

It's a deeply personal experience designed to help you see your whole picture — so your next steps come from alignment, not guesswork.

Think of it as a GPS for your life.

Every meaningful journey begins with two coordinates: your current location and your desired destination. Without both, you can't chart a reliable path forward.

The Clarity Sequence gives you both:

- Assessment—your current location. A structured, compassionate lens through which to view your life as a whole, revealing patterns, pressures, and possibilities that might otherwise stay hidden.

- Aspirations — your desired destination. A guided process to articulate what you truly want to feel, experience, and create in your next chapter.

You can't navigate to your joy using someone else's map.

You have to understand your own terrain—the inner landscape that has shaped where you are today and the desires calling you forward.

This is that moment.

Your next step on the path to joy begins here. Scan the QR code below or visit:

https://modernconsciousness.com/clarity-sequence/

You'll also find free tools and other resources at:

https://modernconsciousness.com/

about the author

Stacie Shifflett is the creator of *Elevate Your Life*® and founder of *Modern Consciousness*®, a movement dedicated to helping people live with greater clarity, alignment, and joy. Through her signature program, she guides others to chart their own *Treasure Map to Joy*™ — a personal framework for rediscovering purpose and fulfillment in everyday life.

You can learn more about Stacie here:

https://modernconsciousness.com/about-me/